Norman Shields writes with wide and continuing experience of teaching Christian ethics at Bible and theological colleges at home and overseas. His new book reflects the work of a clear thinker and lucid writer, and students will particularly appreciate the skill with which he presents his material in a form that is easily recalled.

Committed to the unique authority of Scripture, he explores the ethical perspectives of the patriarchal, Mosaic, prophetic and wisdom traditions before moving to a fine exposition of 'Christ's law'. The author interprets this as an applied expansion of the Old Testament's two basic absolutes (loving the Lord and our neighbour) as they figure prominently in the teaching of Jesus as well as in Paul and the other New Testament writers. Although intentionally confined to the relevant biblical material, the book helpfully relates its teaching to contemporary life in a post-modernist society with its rapidly declining moral standards. This fine book forcefully reminds its readers that the Lord who sets high moral standards for his children, generously provides those resources which make grateful obedience a daily reality.

Dr. Raymond Brown,
formerly Principal, Spurgeon's College, London

When Kathy arrived at her ethics course at college, the textbook explained that there are two approaches to morality: supernaturalistic theories, which base morality on God, and naturalistic theories which try to derive morality apart from God. The textbook then excluded supernaturalistic theories from its discussion. When Kathy asked why, her lecturer replied, 'We don't have time for superstitions around here.' Kathy's experience illustrates what Christian people are up against in our relativistic society. Increasingly 'values' are cut off from their objective or absolute moorings. This is why Norman Shields has done us such great service by expressing with his usual clarity and precision the biblical framework of biblical ethics. He provides the compass we need to find our way through today's moral maze. I recommend it most warmly.

Liam Goligher
Duke Street Baptist Church, Richmond, England

We live in a postmodern society where the very concept of truth is at a discount. In this situation, many people today consider it impossible (or arrogant) to suggest that we can distinguish between good and bad or right and wrong. Above all, our western society has reached the point where there is no longer any consensus of opinion on moral and ethical matters which for hundred of years have remained unchallenged. Given this moral vacuum it is good to be directed towards the Bible as the foundation for all that we think and say and do. Further study in Christian ethics is . . . . s time and this book is to be welcomed

Dr. A.T.B. McGowan
ological College, Dingwall, Scotland

At a time when the sharpest challenges to the Christian faith are frequently ethical rather than theological, and when fewer and fewer members of worshipping congregations have been raised in a Christian environment, books which help Christians grapple with ethical issues are a literal Godsend. Norman Shields' primer on Biblical ethics is a valuable starting point in helping believers of all stages of faith think biblically about how to live out their faith in a pagan environment. His survey chapters are comprehensive, balanced and direct, and regularly indicate some of the more obvious current applications. To put this book in the hands of a new Christian of any age would be a major contribution to their Christian maturity. I commend it heartily.

Dr. Bruce Milne
Senior Minister, First Baptist Church
Vancouver, Canada

Eager to do what is good

What the Bible teaches about Ethics

Norman A Shields

Christian Focus

© Norman A. Shields

ISBN 1 85792 625 0

Published in 2001
by Christian Focus Publications, Geanies House,
Fearn, Ross-shire, IV20 1TW, Great Britain

Cover design by Alister MacInnes

Printed and bound in Great Britain by
The Guernsey Press Co. Ltd., Guernsey, Channel Islands

Contents

This study is dedicated to my wife, Joan,
who for nearly half a century has constantly encouraged me
in the Lord's work, both in West Africa and in Ireland,
and to our children,
Dermot, Michael, Rosemary and Peter,
their spouses and families

Foreword

I am grateful for the stimulus Norman Shields' book provides. It has made me recognise afresh the priority of teaching Christian ethics. Ethical teaching tends to be neglected in the church, and particularly in the local church's teaching curriculum. If that is the case, we fall short of the practice of the early Church in its many congregations. Paul wrote of 'the form of teaching to which Christians were entrusted, and to which they gave their wholehearted obedience' (Rom. 6:17). 'The form of teaching' was undoubtedly the summary of Christian ethics, based upon the teaching of our Lord Jesus, given to new Christians to show them how they should live. This was all part of their being set free from sin and becoming slaves to righteousness (Rom. 6:18).

I remember as a student being impressed by the importance of both *kerugma* and *didache*. *Kerugma* sums up the plain statement of the gospel concerning what God has done in the life, death, resurrection and ascension of the Lord Jesus Christ, according to the Scriptures. *Didache* – meaning literally 'teaching' – sums up the ethical instruction that accompanied it. We find this powerfully and simply expressed in the way in which Paul passed on God's truth to the early Christians. First, he delivered the essential truths of the gospel (1 Cor. 15:3-8) and then followed it by instruction about how they should live (1 Thess. 4:1-8).

Out of a desire perhaps to avoid any sort of authoritarianism, we tend to avoid such direct teaching. It is foolish to do so. The one arises from the other, as we see particularly in a letter like that of Paul to the Ephesians. Its first three chapters relate to what it means to be 'in Christ', and the remaining three on what it means to live out the Christian life in the church, the family, and the world.

Nevertheless the teaching of Christian ethics is neither popular nor prominent in contemporary church life. We may wrongly assume that people know how they should behave, or we may skirt sensitive issues out of fear of offending people or appearing negative. A good example is 1 Thessalonians 4:1-8. As a young Christian, I remember receiving teaching on the words, 'It is God's will that you should be sanctified.' I do not remember, however, any teaching that dealt with the words that followed, 'that you should avoid sexual immorality.' What more relevant teaching can there be in our contemporary society? Whether we are young or old we need it.

For Christian believers there are telling reasons for the study of basic Christian ethics. Let me suggest a few.

First, the proper response to grace is gratitude. I remember the thrill of my first appreciation of this truth, enhanced by the New Testament practice of using the same Greek word for both. When the word is used of God, it is grace; and when it is used of us, it is gratitude. What could more clearly express the relationship between the two? Nowhere is this more clearly seen than in Titus 2:11-14, the passage with which Norman Shields begins his book. Significantly, Paul gives ethical instructions in his letter to Titus to different groups found in the church, such as older men and women, young wives and young men. When we are grateful to God for his grace in his Son, we long to know how we may live to please him. Christian ethics shows us how.

Second, our proper response to God's love is to love him in return. This love, however, is neither sentimental nor a matter of mere words. It is a love seen in obedience. Loving God, we find ourselves asking, 'How may I show it?' The New Testament's answer is not in doubt! By the obedience of our lives to his Word.

Third, while we do not obtain salvation by following the example of our Lord Jesus, once we have obtained salvation through faith in him, he becomes our example in everything. When Peter proclaimed the good news to Cornelius, he summarized the ministry of the Lord Jesus. Part of that summary included the words 'he went around doing good' (Acts 10:38). The Good Samaritan exemplified the Christian ethic, as did the early church as it looked after the poor and the deprived.

Fourth, the proof of faith is good works. James' teaching and emphasis are not contrary to Paul's. Paul's concern is how we first become Christians: it is through grace by faith alone. James' concern is how we may know and demonstrate that we have become Christians: it is through good works produced in our lives by God's Spirit. As it has been well put, when we have returned home like the prodigal son, we must go out like the good Samaritan.

Fifth, Christian ethics and holiness go hand in hand. God's call to every believer is that given to the Jews in the Old Testament and to all Christian believers in the New: 'Be holy, because I am holy' (1 Peter 1:16). Justification leads to sanctification. To be holy is to be like God who cares for the widow, the poor and the needy.

Our appreciation and profit from Norman Shields' excellent little book will be immeasurably increased if we come to it with these compelling reasons for the study of Christian ethics.

Derek Prime

For the grace of God that brings salvation has appeared to all men. It teaches us to say "No" to ungodliness and worldly passions, and to live self-controlled, upright and godly lives in this present age, while we wait for the blessed hope – the glorious appearing of our great God and Saviour, Jesus Christ, who gave himself for us to redeem us from all wickedness and to purify for himself a people that are his very own, *eager to do what is good* (Titus 2:11-14).

Preface

When, in the 1950s I served as Principal of the Qua Iboe Church Bible College in what was then Eastern Nigeria, I developed a course in Christian ethics. This began where all Christian study should begin, that is, in the Bible itself. It went on to discuss the application of biblical principles to some of the practical ethical problems then confronting Christians in their day-to-day living.

From the late 1960s till 1990 I taught Christian ethics in the Irish Baptist College in Belfast. There the course was further developed as new issues arose in society and in church life. Since retirement in 1990 I have continued to teach the subject as a visiting lecturer at the Irish Baptist College and also at the Belfast Bible College.

The present volume is based on the biblical section of these courses. It has been and remains my custom to begin every course on ethics with an overview of what the various sections of Scripture have to say on the subject. I do this because I feel that it is vital that in this age of biblical illiteracy, Christians, and in particular those who are training for ministry or mission, acquire a sound biblical base from which to face the confusing practical problems of the modern world. This volume will, I trust, help students and other readers to acquire that base.

They should then, as Paul put it, be able 'to say "No" to ungodliness and worldly passions, and to live self-controlled, upright and godly lives in this present age' (Tit. 2:12).

My warmest thanks are due to friends who over many years have contributed to the emergence of this book. The first is the late Percy Eyres, who taught Christian Ethics at London Bible College and whose devotion to the Lord and enthusiasm for his subject did much to stimulate my interest in and love for Christian Ethics.

The second is David Kingdon, the former principal of the Irish Baptist College, who in 1998/9 carefully edited the text of *Eager to do what is good* and supplied the study questions, which appear on pages 171-175.

I am deeply grateful to the Rev. Derek Prime for honouring me by writing a foreword for the book and to Drs Bruce Milne, Raymond Brown and A.T. B. McGowan and the Rev. Liam Goligher for the commendations they have provided. Thanks also to Billy and Irene Harrison both of whom have kindly read and checked the text.

I greatly appreciate the fact that Christian Focus Publications accepted my script and also the work their managing editor, Malcolm Maclean, and his staff have put into editing, checking and presenting *Eager to do what is good* in this attractive form.

As these studies are published, it is my prayerful hope that the Lord will use them to the benefit of everyone who reads them.

The fulfilment of Paul's instruction to his friends in the Church at Ephesus should be our aim today:

Walk in a manner worthy of the calling with which you have been called, with all humility and gentleness, with patience, showing forbearance to one another in love, being diligent to preserve the unity of the Spirit in the bond of peace (Eph. 4:1-3, NASB).

1

Ethics today

The English words, ethics, ethical, etc., derive from the Greek *'ethos'* meaning custom, habit or conduct. The science of ethics, which is usually treated as a sub-section of philosophy, seeks to evaluate human conduct and the rules and principles that are used to control it.

The English words, moral, morals, morality, etc. have similar meaning but are derived from the Latin, *'mos, mores'* meaning habit, custom, manner of living etc.

Ethics is concerned with conscious and purposeful behaviour and with the obligations and rules that relate to it. It aims to discover what factors make actions good or bad, right or wrong both for individuals and for social groups. It is concerned with both theory and with practice. Ethicists theorise about what *ought* to be done and then, with varying degrees of success, attempt to show *how* their theories can be worked out in practice.

They focus their attention not just on overt actions but also on what goes on in the minds of those who perform them. Their emphases are highlighted by the vocabulary they use.

The vocabulary of ethical study

1. Right and wrong
These terms assume comparison with some standard of morality – customary, traditional, social, legal, religious or whatever – outside of the action being judged. The idea of a 'moral standard' has produced a number of interesting theories, some of which are briefly introduced below.

2. Good and bad (evil)
To judge an action good or bad goes beyond its mere rightness or wrongness. Such judgment relates to the quality of the action and

13

often at the same time to the quality of the person performing it. His inner state of mind, his desires, motives, intentions, etc. are either approved or censured. An action can be right in the sense that it conforms to a rule but, if the motives are selfish or unworthy, it is not a good action.

In the New Testament the Pharisees gave alms to the poor. Jesus called what they did 'acts of righteousness' (Matt. 6:1). They were doing what was right but their actions were not good because their motive was not to help the poor but to call public attention to themselves.

3. Motivation

Motives are the *desires* and the *intentions* that move a person to action. *Desire* is an inner awareness of some goal which, if it were to be achieved, would make the individual concerned happy or bring him satisfaction or a feeling of being righteous. *Intention* has in view the result we hope to achieve through an action. A good *intention* can make an action more valuable than it otherwise would have been but it cannot turn a bad or immoral action into a good one.

4. Obligation/duty

This is what is *due* by the individual in order to meet some moral necessity. It could be duty in relation to a code of ethical behaviour – a moral standard – imposed by custom or religion and in many cases by accompanying sanctions, or in relation to the inner promptings of what is known as conscience or to both together.

5. Conscience

This is a faculty within us which judges our actions or our intended actions and which seeks to direct us towards right actions. It is an aspect of the cognitive mind and depends on knowledge to function properly. (Our word, conscience, combines the Latin *cum*, meaning 'together with' and *scientia*, meaning 'knowledge'.) Conscience is thus knowledge based and needs education if it is to function properly. Normally through the influences of families, peer groups and wider communities it is educated to socially accepted standards that may or may not have an active or a latent religious content.

From a Christian standpoint it needs to be said that conscience is not of itself the voice of God. It can be and often is the channel through which God does speak. It also needs to be pointed out that, as Paul makes clear, it can be seared and give misleading judgements; it can even be silenced.

Secular Approaches to Ethics

In the modern world there is much confusion about the existence of and the difference between right and wrong. Study of such matters is approached from several different standpoints. For example,

1. Rationalism

This assumes that man's reasoning powers are fully adequate to enable him to make right decisions about his behaviour. It was on this assumption that the ancient Greek philosopher, Socrates, enunciated the dictum, 'knowledge is virtue.' He argued that gaining knowledge by education is the key to virtuous living.

In the Christian era Greek 'rationalism' was largely displaced by an acceptance on the part of the philosophers and doctors of morality (mainly clerics) of biblical absolutes. The Enlightenment of the eighteenth century, brought a change to the intellectual climate by introducing the belief that knowledge and truth are ascertained by rational thought rather than by supernatural divine revelation. This became the dominant philosophy of the nineteenth and early twentieth centuries (the Modernist period). The German philosopher, Immanuel Kant (1724–1804), for example, believed that people were rational and autonomous. His *categorical imperative*, 'Act only on that maxim which you can at the same time will to become a universal law,' is famous. To decide if an action (e.g., stealing) is moral a person should think of what would happen if everyone did it. His own rational thought would tell him that it is immoral to steal.

Many modern rationalists view ethics as an aspect of evolution. Man's conduct is thought to have developed in parallel with the evolution of his physical and psychological natures. In the process his behaviour is constantly improving and progressing towards perfection. This idea is hardly justified by the violent history of the twentieth century.

2. Existential relativism

The second half of the twentieth century was dominated by what is known as existentialism, a philosophy that finds truth and reality in the experience of the moment rather than as the product of history or reason. It grew out of the widespread sense of hopelessness and despair that followed World War II and the advent of nuclear weapons. As the so-called 'cold war' between the West and the Soviet Bloc countries developed many people concluded that the nuclear threat was such as would destroy humanity and possibly even the earth itself. The horrible word 'omnicide', meaning the death of everything living, was coined.

With such a prospect there seemed no point in worrying about moral standards or about tomorrow. Tomorrow might not happen so the best thing would be to make the most of the present. Thus the Epicurean approach to life – 'Eat, drink and be merry for tomorrow we die' – came back with a vengeance. The individual was seen as a free agent set in a seemingly meaningless universe. He finds meaning only as he makes use of the moment of time of which he was assured, namely the moment that actually existed as he thought or spoke. That moment alone had real existence (hence the designation, Existentialism) and in it the individual was regarded as having complete freedom to control his own life.

Such a philosophy admits of no moral obligation, no goals, no models to be copied, no ideals to which an individual is obliged to conform. Ethics, it argues, can only describe or analyse moral concepts but cannot even attempt to define what morality should be. Man is to be himself and do his own thing! If other individuals do different things so be it! Morality is then *relative* to each person or, on a broader canvas, to each particular cultural unit.

Philosophers like Jean Paul Sartre (1905-1980) believed that the individual must create his own moral code and is only responsible to himself. He must not believe in a supreme God to whom he is responsible or in absolutes of right or wrong in human behaviour. Morality is entirely relative to the interest of the individual or the group in the situation existing at the moment. Western education has been considerably influenced by these ideas and now tends to be 'value-neutral' in matters ethical – children are often left in a moral vacuum!

Relativists, who say that there are no absolutes, actually contradict themselves, because the assertion that there are no absolute laws is itself absolute – it is a statement that admits of no alternatives or exceptions. In addition they make it impossible to measure or evaluate any action and make concepts such as better or worse, higher or lower, progress or regress, meaningless. This is because by denying the existence of absolutes they deprive themselves and their followers of an independent measuring rod and without such a rod there can be no measuring at all.

3. Postmodernism

This is the philosophy that dominates thought in the Western world at the end of the twentieth and the beginning of the twenty-first centuries. It goes beyond rationalism in that it discards not just biblical revelation but also the ability of our reasoning powers to arrive at truth. Like relativism it affects the way people live. It influences education and the media. It questions and undermines traditional values, whatever their source, and it challenges and dismisses Christian teaching and Christian absolutes. It pervades modern society and, whether we like it or not, it influences our children and our grandchildren and it probably influences each one of us to some degree.

In the eighteenth and nineteenth centuries The Enlightenment put reason rather than the authority of rulers and prelates on the philosophical throne. People, it was argued, could reason things out for themselves and, with few exceptions, felt no need of God or of religious authority to justify or judge their actions or to guarantee their standards and ideals. Scientific discovery and secular attitudes advanced apace. Liberal thinkers questioned the authority of Scripture and made it subject to the discoveries of science, which, as was the case with Darwinian evolution, were often accepted without question. This was 'modernity' or 'Modernism'.

Science claimed to give the world solid objective facts (i.e., facts that are regarded as true irrespective of what an individual subject might think of them). But as the twentieth century advanced the emphasis shifted to the opinion of the subject whose ideas were being expressed. Truth is now presented as subjective (i.e., as a matter of what you or I or anyone else thinks it to be). Nothing is universally true and applicable to all situations or in all times. Everything is relative to a particular subject in his or her present situation.

Some postmodernists go as far as to say that there is no such thing as truth. All we have or can have are interpretations, your interpretation, my interpretation and the other person's interpretation. The emphasis is not on reality but on interpretation, on the interpreter rather than on truth. The 1960s' drug using hippies' interpretations of life and its values or those of the Hindu guru or the African shaman are as valid as those of the great saints of Christendom. Each spoke or speaks the truth as he sees it in his own situation and nothing that any one of them says is universally true or valid.

There is no belief in divine revelation, no belief that God has set parameters for human behaviour. The biblical basis of morality has been swept away. Every belief, every moral obligation is purely a matter of individual choice. Belief and moral practice are thus entirely relative and one person's interpretation of these things is as valid as that of anyone else.

Self-autonomy is at the heart of this philosophy – no-one, no set of laws can tell me what I should or should not do – 'I am my own master.' What matters for the postmodernist is that the individual is free of all rules and free to make his or her own choices and to find personal happiness and fulfilment as he or she pleases. Each one should therefore seek success and prosperity without the restrictions imposed by any laws or rules, religious or otherwise. Virtues like humility and self-sacrifice are at a discount. 'Go for it' is the motto of many.

Theories about Moral Standards

1. Fittingness Theories

These say that the rightness or wrongness of an action (or of a contemplated action) depends on how it fits in with some factor or with some set of factors outside of itself. Technically these are known as 'deontological' theories, a designation that derives from the Greek word, *deon*, meaning what is needful, due or proper.

In general the factor or factors with which actions are compared and by which they are judged are of two types. They involve *either* a rule or a set of rules (laws) *or* the demands of the specific situation in which an action takes place. On this view each person is regarded as under a duty to act in a way that harmonises with a rule or with the needs of a situation.

i) Fitting rules or laws

Throughout history people have understood the moral standard to which they had to conform as a body of laws. The ancient laws of Hammurabi (around 1800 BC) are one of the earliest known examples of codified law. The laws of Moses came some 550 or 600 years later.

a) Customary and national laws. For many people morality is simply a matter of the customs and traditions that have become essential aspects of life in a particular community. Everyone is expected to conform to these patterns of behaviour, which are known as customary laws. In most African societies, for example, customary law prevents a wife from inheriting the property of her husband. Communities enforce such laws by imposing punishments on or by ostracising those who rebel against them.

Religious communities have laws, which they tend to regard as originating with a deity. Jews find them in the Mosaic laws of the Old Testament and in the Talmud, while Muslims use the Koran. Christians see them as laws of God and of Christ as revealed in the Bible.

Modern states have developed national laws, which require their citizens to behave in particular ways, like paying taxes or

driving vehicles on either the right-hand or the left-hand side of
the road. Those who break these laws are liable to some form of
punishment. What must be recognised by Christians is that
obeying such laws is not the same as obeying God's laws. To put
it another way, what is legal is not always moral and what is
biblically moral is often out of harmony with either cultural
traditions, customary law or national law.

b) Natural law. Some thinkers, who do not acknowledge that
man's moral responsibilities arise before God, say that laws about
behaviour are written in the human heart as part of what they call
'the nature of things.'

Scripture has, of course, a doctrine of law as a deposit put into
human nature by God – 'When Gentiles, who do not possess the
law (i.e., God's law), do by nature what the law requires ... they
show that what the law requires is written on their hearts, while
their conscience also bears witness and their conflicting thoughts
accuse or perhaps excuse them ...' (Rom. 2:14-16, RSV).
Understood in this Pauline sense as a benefit bestowed by the
Creator on all mankind, natural law along with a multitude of
other providences, like the restraining influence of the Roman
Empire, were and are an integral part of what theologians call
'common grace'. As Paul puts it 'the one who now holds it
(lawlessness) back will continue to do so till he/it (probably the
Roman emperor and/or Roman law and order) is taken out of the
way' (2 Thes. 2:7). Without such influences of grace there could
be no order in society and human life would degenerate into total
and intolerable anarchy.

Roman Catholics generally make more of natural law than
Protestants do. They tend to follow Thomas Aquinas (1225-1274),
who taught that human reason could lead men from the created
world to a 'First Cause' and so to God. His 'natural theology' has
been extended to ethics in the form of 'natural law'.

Catholicism insists that natural law is of universal validity,
unchanging and unchangeable and readily recognised by men, the
law written on the heart and transmitted from generation to
generation. Men everywhere are regarded as having an innate

capacity enabling them to recognise and pursue goodness and to reject evil. In Catholic thought natural law acts, then, as an authority additional to Scripture and church tradition.

Natural law tends, however, to be expressed in rather vague generalisations, often focusing on rights like the right to life or to justice, concepts which are often difficult to apply specifically to the personal and moral problems ordinary men and women have to face. At the same time emphasis on rights can encourage a selfish pursuit of one's own or one's community's rights to the neglect of the duty to uphold the rights of others. The more direct guidance of absolute laws and of universal principles is needed.

ii) Fitting specific situations (situation ethics)

Those who adopt this view are essentially existentialists and regard an action as right or wrong, on the basis of how it does or does not fit the situation that exists at the moment at hand. What matters ethically is the way we react to the circumstances of that situation. The result is an *individualistic* 'born-of-the-situation' ethic that can ignore all other standards of morality. Situation ethics side-steps and in the end destroys all the inherited wisdom of the past. No-one can be guided by a custom, a rule, a law or by an example from earlier times. Everyone does what he thinks is right in the situation of the moment.

On the situation ethics theory the individual is the final judge of what is right and the basis of both *social and biblical* morality is destroyed. Society can neither be commended nor condemned because there is no standard by which it can be judged.

Some professed Christians have adopted a slightly modified 'situation ethic' position. They argue that, even if it is found in Scripture, no rule or law other than that of love, should be allowed to dominate a carefully taken judgment based on the circumstances of a particular situation. The insistence that love is an absolute requirement appears to give this view a Christian twist. But it seems to say that if a person's instant assessment of a situation means that he murder or commit adultery, that he steal or bear false witness, he is acting correctly *as long as he is sure that he is acting in love!*

Despite its high-sounding emphasis on love, this view does not and cannot tell us what love is or how it should express itself. A set of values or laws that defines what is good and right is needed before anyone or any group of people can know what to do *in love* in a specific situation.

For the Christian *love is defined by biblical values and biblical laws*. Those values require certain attitudes and actions like giving practical care to neighbours. They rule out actions that could harm others. The idea of love without such definition being the standard of morality is inadequate and essentially unchristian.

2. Consequentialist (Utilitarian) Theories

These take several forms but in general say that an action's rightness or goodness is to be judged by its *consequence(s)*, that is, by what it achieves. Actual results are more important than intended ones. Right actions are those that are useful (have utility) in producing ends thought to be good (hence the name Utilitarianism). Good consequences are thought of in terms of maximising human wellbeing, but anticipating or measuring this is virtually impossible. Translating it into moral obligation is equally difficult.

On these theories good consequences are thought of in a variety of ways. They can:

- *focus on what is useful for oneself.* This is Egotistic or Egotistical Utilitarianism because it is concerned only with the achievement of *personal* benefit or personal happiness

- *be concerned with what benefits most people.* This is Altruistic Utilitarianism and is generally regarded as more attractive than the egotistical variety, because it tends to inject something of the idea of 'justice for all' into that of utility.

- *be directed at gaining pleasure.* This is called Hedonistic Utilitarianism. It can be either egotistical (the only worthwhile consequence is one's own pleasure) or altruistic (the good consequence is the pleasure of others).

- *aim to fulfil high ideals.* This is known as Idealistic Utilitarianism. Its advocates concern themselves with ensuring that their actions and those of others are such as express ideals like love, virtue, beauty etc.

- *accept a minimum number of rules.* There are some, who try to improve the image of consequentialist ethics by using a small number of moral rules that seek to limit self-indulgence and/or injustice. These are called 'rule-utilitarians'

The above categories are not watertight - there is often a degree of overlap among them. A person can at one point be egotistical and at another altruistic. He can be at one point hedonistic and at another idealistic. He may be basically utilitarian and yet affirm some rules to ensure that life does not descend into total anarchy.

And there are Christians who seem to think of God, not merely as a Sovereign to whom they must render account, but as One who simply helps them achieve their own goals—pass exams, get a good job and a good income, etc., etc. They might profess to be bound by divine law but in practice they are inconsistent and essentially utilitarian!

Utilitarianism can negate justice

By themselves consequentialist or utilitarian theories tend to encourage the idea that *'the end justifies the means.'* Thus, if an action that in itself would be unjust or otherwise unacceptable, can be *useful* in producing a desirable end, it is thought to be right. What works for an individual or for a social group is regarded as morally right!

On utilitarian premises an innocent person, for example, could be punished on a trumped up charge in order to deter others and, if some deterrence occurred, the punishment would be adjudged useful and right. On other theories such an action would be regarded as a serious denial of justice and grossly immoral. For the Utilitarian what is disliked (justice) can be ignored, while what is favoured (utility) is encouraged!

Utilitarianism falls short of the Christian ideal

The lack of emphasis on moral absolutes and on justice is good reason for regarding consequentialist or utilitarian theories as inadequate and less than Christian.

Conclusion

Morality in Western society has become thoroughly secularised at the end of the twentieth and the beginning of the twenty-first centuries. Moral absolutes have been replaced by the ambivalent values of the individual and by a cult of self-autonomy and self-realisation, which Dr Jonathan Sachs, the Chief Rabbi of Great Britain, has characterised as 'moral cop-out' (The Times, 23/1/99). Man, fallen man indeed, is central as every man does 'as he sees fit' (Deut. 12:8, Jud. 17:6, KJV, 'does what is right in his own eyes').

2

The backdrop to biblical ethics

Biblical ethics arises within the context of belief in God the Lord, Jehovah or Yahweh, as his Hebrew name can be transliterated. It is known as 'Theological Ethics' because the Bible presents it as the standard given to men by God *(theos* is the Greek word for God). Biblical Ethics both expresses God's own character and indicates the behaviour he wants to see in his creatures and especially in those who become his people.

Before we immerse ourselves in a study of how ethical teaching developed in the Bible it will be wise to look briefly at the theological backdrop of human sinfulness and of God's grace in salvation that lies behind the teaching of his word about good behaviour.

Scripture opens with an account of how God created and gave life to the human race (Gen. 1:26, 27; 2:7). It goes on to show how our first parents, Adam and Eve, succumbed to temptation and fell into sin. Because they were enticed by an agent external to themselves we can say that sin was an intrusion into human life. The effect of that happening was devastating and extends throughout the human race to this day, as the apostle, Paul, makes absolutely clear:

.... sin entered the world through one man and death through sin, and in this way death came to all men ... the many died by the trespass of the one man ... the result of one trespass was condemnation for all men ... through the disobedience of the one man many were made sinners (Rom. 5:12, 15, 18, 19).

The nature of sin

Scripture presents sin as behaviour out of harmony with what God requires of his creatures. It arises both in our thoughts and in our actions and also in our failures, in what we omit to think or do.

25

We are guilty of sins of omission as well as of commission.

The nature of sin is shown by the Hebrew and Greek words Scripture uses to refer to it. The various terms can, however, be brought together into three groups to show that sin is:

1. Failure before God

The first set of words (Hebrew *chattah* and Greek *hamartia*) define sin as 'falling short' of a standard or as 'missing' a target. The nouns are usually translated into English as 'sin/sins' and the associated verbs as 'to sin'. They are general words for shortcoming before God. Men fail to meet God's requirements to love and be loyal to him, to worship and serve him and to behave in ways that please him.

In the Old Testament, ritual failures and civil offences as well as moral aberrations were such shortcomings and were designated 'sins'. The word was thus used with a much wider meaning than is normal today, when its focus following that of the New Testament is exclusively on moral failures.

In the Gospels we read, however, of Pharisees using the words sin and sinner of fellow Jews who did not belong to and keep the rules of their particular sect. They were, of course, arrogantly self-righteous and would neither receive food from nor eat with such people and criticised Jesus for doing so. He totally rejected their criticism. He also rejected their whole system, which added a multitude of petty extra laws or traditions to those of Moses and made observance of their rules the basis of acceptance before God. He told them that he had come not to call the righteous (i.e., the Pharisees who thought themselves righteous), but sinners to repentance (Mark 2:15-17).

2. Rebellion against God

This group of words (Hebrew *pesha'* and the Greek *anomia*, *parabasis* and *epithumia*) focuses on the tendency of men to cross over or transgress boundaries set by God. Where he says, 'You shall not' man says 'I will' and does what he wills! He is a transgressor, a trespasser, a lawless person who lusts for or desires what is forbidden. As such a person David prayed for God's forgiveness – 'blot out my transgressions' (Ps. 51:1). The apostles wrote of transgression as a violation of law – 'Everyone who sins breaks the law; in fact, sin is lawlessness' (1 John 3:4, cf. Rom. 4:15, Jas. 2:9,11).

3. Perversion of heart and character

In the Old Testament the Hebrew word is *'awon* and in the New the Greek one is *adikia*. In both, the meaning is variously rendered as 'iniquity', 'unrighteousness', 'wickedness' or 'evil'. They indicate that man is twisted in his innermost being. He is perverse in his attitudes and his desires and by nature is off the straight and narrow path of righteousness. He is opposed to God's standards and is inwardly corrupt. Every single individual is affected in every aspect of his or her life. As our Lord put it, men are 'evil' (Luke 11:13, cf. Rom. 3:23; 5:12-19).

On a number of occasions we find these three ideas, or two of them, linked together. The classic instance is David's prayer in Psalm 51. He prayed for cleansing from his iniquities and his sins and sought forgiveness for his transgressions:

> Have mercy on me, O God ...
>   blot out my *transgressions*.
> Wash away all my *iniquity*
>   and cleanse me from my *sin*.
> For I know my transgressions,
>   and my sin is always before me
>   (Ps. 51:1-3, cf. Exod. 34:7; Job 13:23; Isa. 59:2-3, 12).

Sin is, then, a basic condition of the human heart, a perversity that produces transgressions and a host of moral failures. Initially it is a hereditary or natural condition passed from parents to child. It is thus a matter of what we are – of our state. We are all born sinners with iniquity in our hearts.

However the fact that we are born sinners does not mean that we can avoid taking responsibility for our actions. Quite the reverse is the case. Sin is also an active condition in which the sinner participates. He is not merely ill or deformed or in need of psychiatric treatment; he is a morally responsible person accountable before God for all his actions. Thus David recognised his responsibility before God and God's right to impose appropriate justice on him as a sinner.

> Against you, you only, have I sinned
>   and done what is evil in your sight, so that
> You are proved right when you speak
>   and justified when you judge (Ps. 51:4).

4. Inherent selfishness

Old and New Testaments unite to affirm that man's first duty is to love the Lord with his entire being, to put God first in his life and to give priority to God's kingdom (Deut. 6:5; Matt. 6:33; Col. 3:1). By nature men do not do this but instead put self at the centre of their thinking and living. They are essentially self-centred and this means that in considerable measure they put themselves in opposition to God. When they choose to disobey God, whether by neglecting his commands or by deliberately trespassing against them, they choose to please self rather than God. Self is the supreme object of their affection and the supreme end for which they live.

Selfishness expresses itself in unbelief before God. Man in a right relationship with God would receive and accept whatever God reveals to him as vested with divine authority and binding on his own life. He would, to use John's words, 'walk in the light.' In fact, however, he loves darkness more than light – he rejects spiritual light (John 3:19-20; cf. Rom. 1:26-28) and doesn't readily believe or act on what God has been pleased to reveal. He prefers his own ideas and lives in unbelief. Such unbelief together with the selfishness it expresses is sin (John 16:9).

The Shorter Catechism based on the Westminster Confession of Faith defined sin in terms of failure before God's law. In it sin is defined as 'any want of conformity unto or transgression of the Law of God'. Dr. E. F. Kevan offered a definition, which takes account of the selfishness at the heart of sin and includes most of what Scripture affirms: 'Any attitude of indifference, disobedience or unbelief to the will of God as revealed in Law or Gospel, whether the attitude expresses itself in thought, word, deed or settled disposition' (from unpublished notes).

The universality of sin

Scripture clearly teaches that sin, both as a state of the heart and as acts of the will, is a universal phenomena. All men without exception are affected.

The sinful condition of the human heart and the wickednesses that flow from it emerged early. We read that just prior to the Flood, 'The LORD saw how great man's wickedness on the earth had become, and that every inclination of the thoughts of his heart was only evil all the time' (Gen. 6:5). Solomon's great prayer at the dedication of the temple included the words, 'there is no-one who does not sin.' Later Jeremiah found it necessary to say, 'The heart is deceitful above all things and beyond cure' (Jer. 17:9). Jesus himself affirmed the fact that men are essentially evil in nature, 'If you then, though you *are evil...*' (Luke 11:13). Paul quoting loosely from several Psalms says,

There is no-one righteous, not even one;
  there is no-one who understands,
  no-one who seeks God.
All have turned away,
  they have together become worthless;
there is no one who does good, not even one. ...
for all have sinned and fall short of the glory of God
  (Rom. 3:10-18, 23, cf. Job 14:1-4; Pss. 14, 53, 58:3, 143:2;
          Prov. 20:9; Ecc. 7:20; Gal. 3:22; 1 John 1:8).

Whenever Scripture proclaims that all men are under condemnation and liable to divine wrath it is asserting the universality of sin – all deserve punishment because all men are sinners and have committed sin. As John puts it, 'whoever rejects the Son will not see life, for God's wrath remains on him (John 3:36, cf. 3:18; Eph. 2:3; 1 John 5:19; Rom. 5:12-14). Similarly passages which affirm that God in Christ had to save the world assume that all the inhabitants of the world are sinners who need redemption. God loved the world and gave his only Son in order to provide a way of escape from perdition for those who would believe in him. Jesus came to save men rather than to condemn them (John 3:16, 18, 36; 6:50; 12:47; Acts 4:12; 17:30).

Around the world people have an innate sense of sin and of guilt. They resort to priests and to sacrificial offerings, aiming to rid themselves of the penalties they feel they deserve because of their sins. Christians, who are growing in grace, realise more and more that their hearts are evil and that they have transgressed against the Lord and still do so. Experience unites, then, with the clear testimony of Scripture to affirm that sin is universal – 'there is none righteous, no, not one.'

The effects of sin

Scripture indicates a number of significant ways in which sin affects human beings both in terms of this life and of the prospects for the life to come.

1. Separation from God
The story of the Fall climaxes with Adam and Eve being banished from the Garden of Eden and from the tree of life, and therefore from eternal life (Gen. 3:22). No more would a holy God walk and talk with man in the garden. A relationship arising from creation was broken; man was separated from his Maker.

The rest of Scripture confirms this picture. Isaiah said to the Jews of his day, 'Your iniquities have separated you from your God; your sins have hidden his face from you, so that he will not hear' (Isa. 59:2). Jesus conveyed the same idea by speaking of 'the lost' (Luke 15:3-32; 19:10) and by referring to the ultimate separation of eternity 'in hell, where the fire never goes out' (Mark 9:44-48). Paul's description of the unconverted as 'aliens' and 'enemies' (Eph. 2:12) assumes a ruptured relationship between God and his creatures. Man as a sinner is cut off from God and needs someone to mediate in order to restore fellowship with him (John 14:6; 2 Cor. 5:18-21; Eph. 2:18; 1 Tim. 2:5; 1 Pet. 3:18).

2. Depravity of heart
Scripture, as we have seen, witnesses to the corruption, the depravity of human nature. This depravity is 'total' in the sense

that it affects the whole human race and every part of each individual. Man is always subject to the effect of a downward moral gravity and finds himself unable to love and serve God with the single-minded devotion of his entire being. Paul knew this all too well in his own experience and wrote: 'I know that nothing good dwells within me, that is in my flesh. I can will what is right, but I cannot do it. For I do not do the good I want, but the evil I do not want is what I do' (Rom. 7:18-19, NRSV).

Depravity refers to man's lack of essential righteousness and of that total love for God that is demanded of him. He substitutes self for God and worships and serves the creature rather than the Creator (Rom. 1:25). Even his best actions, which by human standards might be called good, are not truly good or righteous before God and do not gain acceptance before him; they are tainted by sinfulness and self-centredness.

We must be careful, however, not to overstate the truth of human depravity. 'Total depravity' does not mean that man is totally depraved but that he is affected by sin in every part of his being. The Bible does not say that every man is as bad as bad can be! It does not teach that men are incapable of doing anything good. Jesus spoke of men knowing how to do good by giving good gifts to their children (Matt. 7:11; Luke 11:13). Paul acknowledged that those who do not know God and who are ignorant of his laws, have an awareness of his demands and a conscience that testifies to what is right or wrong and leaves them without excuse (Rom. 1:19-20; 2:15).

3. Inability to conquer evil

There is no means by which a man can correct his bias towards evil or offset the damage done by the Fall and by his own personal acts of sin. He can no more bring about his own recovery than he can lift himself off the ground by pulling at his shoe laces. Throughout Scripture salvation is a work of God and of God alone. Man is impotent – he can neither cleanse away the impurity of his sinfulness (Jer. 2:22) nor redeem his soul or that of any of his fellows (Ps. 49:7).

In the New Testament man is presented as lost and perishing.

He is dead in trespasses and sins (Eph. 2:1). He is incapable of receiving the things of the Spirit (1 Cor. 2:14) and is without hope and without God (Eph. 2:12-22). He needs someone who will step in and do for him what he cannot do for himself, who will save him from his sinfulness and its consequences. That someone is the Lord Jesus, the one mediator between God and men, the One who gave his life as an exchange-ransom for many (Mark 10:45).

4. Guilt and demerit before God

Sin results in guilt, which Scripture presents mainly in terms of liability before God. The sinner is a debtor under obligation to God and liable to receive punishment. At the same time guilt invests the offender with a negative quality of life, a personal demerit.

From a biblical standpoint guilt involves personal liability for one's thoughts and actions. It is an objective reality, whether the offender is aware of it or not. The Old Testament tells us that God reacts in anger against those who violate his laws (e.g., Ps. 5:4-5). Such offenders are under his curse (Deut. 27:26; Gal. 3:10) and thus liable to his wrath (Nah. 1:2; Rom. 1:18).

At the same time both testaments affirm that God cannot ignore sin or hold the guilty innocent (Exod. 34:7; Num. 14:18; Nah. 1:3-11). Rather he must and will reward every man according to his works (Ps. 62:2; Prov. 24:12; Jer. 32:19; Ezek. 33:20; Matt. 16:27; Rom. 2:6; 2 Cor. 5:10).

The New Testament asserts that God reckons against us (or imputes to us) some aspect of Adam's sin. In introducing sin into the race Adam brought condemnation and death on his entire posterity (Rom. 5:12; 1 Cor. 15:22). Man is therefore under God's wrath from the moment of his conception and independently of any sinful acts he may commit later in his life. As David put it in his great confession (Ps. 51:5):

> Surely I have been a sinner from birth,
>   Sinful from the time my mother conceived me.

Each individual is therefore seen as bringing a sinful nature into the world at birth (original sin). Paul's words in Romans 5:12-21 affirm that we are linked to Adam in terms of racial sinfulness, of guilt and of liability to death and condemnation. In Adam, all are dead and under condemnation and, without exception, need the forgiving and regenerating grace of God.

Even when by the grace of God the Christian has received forgiveness he or she is still the person who committed and who commits sin, and who must always acknowledge personal demerit and guilt. Like Paul each Christian must exclaim, 'Christ Jesus came into the world to save sinners – of whom I am the worst' (1 Tim. 1:15).

5. Liability to receive punishment

Our indebtedness before God brings us into condemnation and makes us liable to receive divine retribution, which operates at two levels:

a) Through the laws of nature. God has built into the created world principles that ensure that men suffer consequences arising from their own sin. If they are lazy and don't work properly the penalty is poverty (e.g., Prov. 20:4). If they pursue foolish and sinful ways, if they allow themselves to become addicted to a damaging habit, they reap what they have sown (Gal. 6:6-8). Sin most surely brings unhappy and deleterious consequences.

b) In acts of divine judgment. God is judge and acts as a judge in relation to his creatures. Some of his judgments bring penalties immediately and some only do so later or in the next life (1 Tim. 5:24). Very quickly David received a judicial punishment of this kind, when the child of his adulterous relationship with Bathsheba was taken from him in death (1 Sam. 12:1-17). Ananias and Sapphira received punishment for their sins in the untimely deaths that overtook them (Acts 5:1-11).

Ultimately all men will give account before God. Judgment will be pronounced on their deeds and rewards and punishments awarded (Num. 14:18; 1 Chr. 10:13; Ps. 11:6; Matt. 16:27; Rom. 2:5-11; 1 Cor. 4:5). Even some of those who know the Lord are liable to be saved only, as we would say, by the skin of their teeth as their unproductive works are burned up (1 Cor. 3:10-15).

The ultimate judicial penalty will be death – 'the soul who sins

... will die' (Ezek. 18:4) – 'the wages of sin is death' (Rom. 6:23).
This can be viewed both as natural and as judicial penalty. Sin
meant that it became natural for men to die and return to the dust
from which their physical nature was created (Gen. 3:19; Ecc.
12:7 and, almost certainly, also Rom. 5:12). But in Romans 5
'death' also embraces spiritual death and its outcome in ultimate
and final separation from God. Because of the Fall the natural or
unregenerate man is dead in his transgressions and sins (Eph. 2:1)
and needs regeneration.

Finally, there is eternal death. This is the consummation of a
godless life as the wrath of God bears down on the sinner and
consigns him or her to outer darkness and everlasting perdition
(Matt. 10:28; 13:40-42; Mark 9:48; 2 Thess. 1:9; Rev. 14:11). In
Revelation 20:14-15 it is called 'the second death'.

Liable to the penalty of eternal death, man is in an awful plight.
He needs a Saviour who bears the penalty of his sin, death included,
on his behalf and who frees him from guilt and condemnation.

Salvation and ethics

Scripture constantly presents the Lord as a God of compassion
and grace. Sin is an offence to him, an offence that his fallen
creatures cannot put right, but from earliest times he disclosed the
fact that he would effect redemption. He would send a Deliverer,
who would be Immanuel or 'God with us' (Isa. 7:14, cf. Matt.
1:23). Thus the Lord God would step into the stream of human
life. By being pierced for our transgressions and crushed for our
iniquities and by taking the punishment that would bring us peace
(Isa. 53:5), Immanuel would free those enslaved by fear of the
death that results from the sin of Adam and from their own sins
(Heb. 2:14,15, cf. Rom. 5:12).

God fulfilled this and other predictions in his one and only
Son, the Lord Jesus Christ, who came to give his life as a ransom
sacrifice for sinful men and women (Mark 10:45). He, Jesus, took
the penalty due to us sinful human beings upon himself – 'he
himself bore (carried) our sins in his own body on the tree' and it
is by his wounds that salvation and healing are effected (1 Pet.

2:24). It is by turning to and believing in him, that is, by coming to him in repentance and faith, that a sinner finds forgiveness and justification before God. As Paul put it, being 'justified through faith' he and his readers and, indeed, believers in every age, 'have peace with God through our Lord Jesus Christ' (Rom. 5:1).

God's saving work in the human heart is not just an insurance policy against eternal punishment. It is essentially a work that brings a transformed lifestyle in the here and now. As Peter put it, Jesus bore our sins in his own body *so that we might die to sins and live for righteousness* (1 Pet. 2:24). In other words the salvation of the individual has an ethical dimension. He or she is meant to die to, and therefore be constantly dead to, sin and committed to righteousness. Each believer in Christ must take on board the implications of Paul's argument in Romans 6:2-4 – 'We died to sin; how can we live in it any longer? ... We are buried with him through baptism into death *in order that*, just as Christ was raised from the dead ... *we too may live a new life.*'

New life for the Christian means transformation by the renewing of the mind and will and a rejection of conformity to the world and its standards (Rom. 12:1, 2). It means adopting the kind of attitudes that controlled our Lord's actions during his life on earth (Phil. 2:5; 1 Pet. 4:1).

It means a changed lifestyle involving, among other things, hatred of what is evil and love for what is good. It means maintaining spiritual fervour in the service of the Lord. It means sharing one's resources with fellow Christians who are in need. It means overcoming evil with good (Rom. 12:9-21).

Such a lifestyle does not come about automatically in the lives of believers. It demands the presence and the controlling power of the Holy Spirit. As Paul told his readers in Galatia, it was by living in or under the control of the Holy Spirit that they would cease from gratifying the desires of their sinful natures (Gal. 5:16). The same apostle insists that Christians must put their whole heart and soul into the business of purifying themselves from moral and spiritual contamination and of perfecting holiness before the Lord (2 Cor. 7:1).

It is with this lifelong task of purifying ourselves (cf. 1 Pet.

1:13-16) and of pursuing holiness that we are concerned in this volume. After a general overview of the emphases of Christian ethics (chapter 3) we will look at Genesis, the Ten Commandments and the prophets and sages of the Old Testament. Then we will seek to highlight the moral teaching of Jesus (what Paul calls 'Christ's Law') as setting out the moral standards to which Christ's followers are ever obligated.

Christians need to remember that to counteract the downward pull of sin in their lives they must have consciences enlightened by the ethical teachings of Jesus. They also need the power that flows from the presence of the Holy Spirit living and working within them to produce his unique fruit – 'love, joy, peace, patience, kindness, goodness, faithfulness, gentleness and self-control' (Gal. 5: 22, 23).

3

Approaching biblical ethics

The studies that follow are based on a conservative evangelical approach to Scripture. Its inspiration, integrity and authority as God's revelation to mankind are assumed. The aims of the studies are, firstly, to discover what God's standards for behaviour were in Bible times and, secondly, to note their relevance for subsequent ages and in particular for ourselves as individual Christians and as Christian communities today.

To set the scene we begin with an introductory survey of biblical ethics.

The moral order from Creation onwards

Scripture opens with God as the creator of the world and of all forms of life. It presents man as the crown of creation and as 'made in God's image' (Gen. 1:27). As such man was and always remains a moral being, one who is responsible to God and whose actions can be judged right or wrong, good or evil on the basis of how they conform to or deviate from his character and from the demands he makes in Scripture.

At creation man was given a number of duties. He was to reproduce his own species in 'one-flesh' marriages (Gen. 1:27-28; 2:24). He was to work in order to gather the fruit of the earth for food and he was expected to rule over other living creatures. These God-given instructions are known as 'creation ordinances' and show that, from the beginning, man was accountable to God for his behaviour. Adam and Eve soon discovered that to be the case, when they disobeyed a divine command and found themselves called to account as a result (Gen. 3). In the next generation their son Cain was held responsible for, and punished for, murdering his brother Abel (Gen. 4).

The Flood (Gen. 6–8) is further testimony to the way in which from earliest times sinful behaviour brought divine retribution. When that had taken place the creation ordinances were repeated and expanded in the instructions given to Noah (Gen. 9:1-17). One of the additional provisions gave permission for animal flesh to be used as human food (v.3). This was subject to the condition that blood was not included in what was eaten. A further emphatic provision strengthened the sanctity of human life by saying that anyone who shed the blood of a human being would have his own blood taken. Thus capital punishment was introduced and the leniency displayed towards Cain was apparently reversed.

The emphasis on an initial universal moral order, based in God's creation of the human race, is implicit in the teachings of our Lord and of Paul. Jesus, for example, affirmed that at the beginning (i.e., in creation) God imposed a moral quality on marriage – he meant it to be permanent (Matt. 19:3-12).

Writing to the Romans, Paul drew attention to the fact that from the creation of the world (i.e., before the law of Moses was given) there was a knowledge of God that carried with it moral responsibility. Because men did not live by the light that had been given to them, God gave them over to their own sinful desires. Gentiles, who in Paul's day did not have the Mosaic law, had the requirements of divine law written in their hearts. Nonetheless, like those who lived before Moses, they will be judged by God (Rom. 1:18–2:16). Later in the same letter Paul argued that, though sin was not taken into account where there was no knowledge of God's law, it and its penalty, death, nevertheless existed before the Mosaic law was given (Rom. 5:12-14). Men were held accountable before God on the basis of moral values written on their hearts (i.e., what is often called 'natural law'). Paul insisted, indeed, that all men, irrespective of race or religion, are personally responsible before God – not one is righteous – 'all have sinned and fall short of the glory of God' (Rom. 3:10, 23).

The law of Moses

After several centuries in Egypt God redeemed Israel from what had become abject slavery. After crossing the Red Sea, they were on their way to a promised land, where they would need a framework of law to govern the various aspects of their life, first in the wilderness and later in the promised land. It is, indeed, at this point in their history that legal language first appears on the pages of the Old Testament. This was necessary because without a framework of law, life in the land would have degenerated into anarchy.

In the teaching of Moses there are *two basic absolute commands*, which in broad terms define how man should relate both to God and to his fellows – 'You shall love the LORD your God with all your heart and with all your soul and with all your strength' (Deut. 6:5) and 'You shall love your neighbour as yourself' (Lev. 19:18).

These absolutes appear in a more detailed form in the Ten Commandments. The first three commands relate specifically to love for God, the fourth has both Godward and manward dimensions and the fifth, while primarily manward, seems also to have a Godward significance. The remaining five are primarily manward but because they were given by God they also involve a Godward dimension – to kill a man is an offence not just against the man but against God.

The Ten Commandments and a group of subsidiary ordinances or judgments were given to Moses at Sinai (Ex. 20–24). Later many other laws were added resulting in the large body of law that came to be known as 'The Law of Moses'. In the process God's revelation was moving forward. He was showing his people more of the sinfulness of sin and more of his own holiness.

The Ten Commandments focused on spiritual and moral issues and were introduced by a divine affirmation – 'I am the LORD your God, who brought you out of Egypt, out of the land of slavery' (Exod. 20:2). The clear implication was that *the commands that followed were given as a code of conduct befitting those whom God had so graciously and so wonderfully redeemed from slavery in Egypt.* The Israelites needed to know how God wanted them to live now that they were free and the law was God's provision to meet that need.

Additionally the law was intended to discourage sin and to

protect the Israelites from it. The giving of the law was followed
by disturbances like thunderings and earthquakes, which brought
fear to the people. Through these God was affirming the
commandments by a sign and was testing the Israelites to ensure
that his fear in their hearts would keep them from sinning (Exod.
20:18-20).

At no point were the Ten Commandments or the rest of the
Mosaic law said to be a means by which Israelites could work to
secure the kind of salvation we meet in the New Testament.
Obedience to God's commands was, however, a condition for the
continued *enjoyment* of the privilege, which resulted from their
redemption from Egypt, namely that of being God's covenant and
treasured people (Exod. 19:3-6).

All ten commandments were developed and applied in the Old
Testament by the addition of subsidiary enactments aimed at
regulating the lives of God's people. While the Israelites often
failed to observe them, they knew they were subject to them and
that they would be held accountable for their disobedience. (We
will examine the commandments in more detail later).

Three distinct categories of law – moral, ceremonial and civil
– can be discerned in the laws Moses was given for Israel. These
are:

1. Moral

This category is primarily concerned with personal conduct and
is strongly emphasised in the Decalogue (i.e., the Ten
Commandments). They in turn are summarised in the two which
Jesus later called the two greatest commandments. They are 'Love
the LORD your God with all your heart and with all your soul and
with all your strength' (Deut. 6:5) and 'You shall love your
neighbour as yourself' (Lev. 19:18).

2. Ceremonial

This category of law was concerned with the Israelites' approach
to God. It showed how fellowship with him was to be maintained
through offerings and service that honoured him. It also provided
means by which barriers to such fellowship, barriers created by
failures (sins) or defilements that marred a person's consecration

to the Lord, could be removed. The Levitical sacrificial system was central to ceremonial law but was valid only in the case of offences committed in ignorance, i.e., shortcomings, mistakes or oversights of a non-deliberate nature (cf. Heb. 9:7). Such sacrifices could not clear the conscience of a worshipper as the sacrifice of Christ does (Heb. 9:14), but they were types or pictures pointing to his sacrifice.

3. Civil

Civil laws were designed to control the social life of God's people in the land he had given to them. They were expressions of what is called 'theocratic (i.e., God's) rule' in the community. These laws carried with them appropriate penalties for those who broke them, whether moral, ceremonial or civil. Murder, adultery, kidnapping and blasphemy carried the death penalty. Acts of theft were punished by requiring the thief to make restitution to the person whose property he had stolen. The restitution could amount to as much as five times what had been stolen (Exod. 22:1).

Fulfilment in Christ

The Mosaic law was important in its day but in the overall divine revelation it was as a body of law primarily applicable to the Old Covenant era, in what the New Testament calls, 'the time then present' (Heb. 9:9). At the same time it illustrated and pointed forward to the work of Christ and to the new law, the law of Christ that he would inaugurate to guide his followers as they would seek to live in harmony with God's will.

The New Testament shows clearly that the law of Moses – moral, ceremonial and civil – was fulfilled in Christ (Matt. 5:17b). It had served its purpose and is not as a body of law binding on Christians except in so far as its moral absolutes were endorsed and re-affirmed by Jesus. That endorsement was primarily in terms of the great commands to love the Lord and to love neighbours and of their expansion in the Ten Commandments.

But on the other hand ceremonial laws, like those relating to clean and unclean food, were abandoned – 'Jesus declared all foods clean' (Mark 7:19, cf. Acts 10:9-16). In overall terms Gentile believers were freed from the burdens of Jewish law, which would include Levitical ceremonial requirements, by the Council of Apostles and others in Jerusalem (Acts 15:24-29). Of supreme importance is the fact that the sacrifice made by Christ was a 'once for all' affair that needs no repetition and that renders the sacrifices of the Levitical system totally redundant (Heb. 10:26).

The civil laws and the penalties that went with them had also served their purpose during the centuries of Israelite/Jewish theocracy. Once independence ceased, the Jews came under the laws of other countries and could only maintain some of their own on a limited local basis. With the coming of Christ and the Christian era, national and spiritual identities were no longer the same. As citizens Christians lived not under the laws of Moses but under those of the Roman Empire and of its subsidiary local administrations. The civil laws of Moses could not be applied and had, in fact, fulfilled their purpose. They had been fulfilled.

Christians live in the age of the New Covenant, inaugurated by the atoning work of Christ. Their primary devotion and obedience must be to him and to his teachings – to his laws. He said:

> Whoever has my commands and obeys them, he is the one who loves me.... If anyone loves me, he will obey my teaching. My Father will love him, and we will come to him and make our home with him. He who does not love me will not obey my teaching. (John 14:21-24).

The law of Christ

Just as the predictions of the prophets about Jesus were fulfilled in his life, death and resurrection so the law in all its aspects was fulfilled in him. Almost certainly this means that God's intention for the whole body of Old Testament law was realised in Christ. It also means that, in the new order he was initiating, it was his teaching, the law of Christ as Paul calls it, which was to be the standard his disciples would be expected to follow.

The law of Christ (1 Cor. 9:21) is not the law of Moses but, while it does embrace love for God and love for neighbours (Matt. 22:37-40; Gal. 5:13, 14), it is a new ethic appropriate to the new kingdom of God. Our Lord said that while the law and the prophets had been preached till the time of John the Baptist, since then in his own ministry the kingdom of God was being proclaimed (Luke 16:16). That proclamation included the laws of the kingdom or in Paul's words, 'the law of Christ.'

The law of Christ provides the Christian with a clear moral standard outside of himself. That standard has two main elements, absolute laws and a number of important principles that provide the basis of moral guidance where absolute laws are not available.

1. Absolute laws

Jesus endorsed each of the Ten Commandments. He directly quoted all except the fourth but his statement, 'the Sabbath was made for man' clearly re-affirmed the principle that one day's rest should follow six days of toil. Thus Jesus incorporated the duties of the Ten Commandments into his law and by doing so placed absolute obligations on his followers.

In some cases Jesus also brought to the fore a deeper meaning of a particular commandment and made it part of the obligation of that commandment. Thus he showed that hating one's brother puts one into a category similar to that of murderers (Matt. 5:21-26). He also made it clear that adultery was not just a matter of an outward physical act but of inward desires – looking lustfully is to commit adultery in the heart (Matt. 5:28). Similarly love for neighbours means loving one's enemies as well as one's friends (Matt. 5:43-47).

Clearly then the law of Christ takes up the abiding essentials of the Old Testament law and adds to them new elements associated with the new kingdom of God. It is the precepts and principles of the kingdom which are the fulfilment of the Old Testament law and that will not 'by any means disappear' (Matt. 5:17-18). In effect Jesus' teachings (the law of Christ) have gathered up into themselves the abiding significance of Old Testament law and have either abrogated it or reinterpreted it for his disciples (see, e.g., Mark 1:41, where by touching a leper he set aside the law of Leviticus 13:45, 46).

Apostolic endorsement of Christ's law

Paul's words, indicating that he was free from Jewish law but not free from God's law, further affirm the binding nature of the teachings of Christ. The apostle saw himself as living 'under Christ's law' (1 Cor. 9:21). To the Galatians he said, 'Carry each other's burdens, and in this way you will fulfil the law of Christ' (Gal. 6:2). For Paul 'the law of Christ' was the law to which he submitted and which he expected his readers to observe. Being under that law he and his readers were not free to do as they pleased (cf. Gal. 5:13-15). They were ruled by the absolutes of Christ's law.

The apostle James had a similar emphasis when he spoke of loving one's neighbour as a keeping of 'the royal law' (Jas. 2:8). Clearly he meant the law given by Christ as king, in effect, 'the law of Christ.'

2. Principles

In many situations in life Christians find that the commands of Jesus do not speak specifically to the problems they face.

In this event the New Testament Scriptures enunciate principles and set goals and make the pursuit of those goals part of a Christian's obligations. Thus the Christian ethic embraces both obedience to the commands of Christ's law and the practical application of New Testament principles to issues not covered by those commands.

In Paul's day, for example, the issue of eating meat which had been offered to an idol was a problem (1 Cor. 8 and 10). Converts to Christianity living in an animistic environment can face that very problem today. However for many people in the West the issue is more likely to be some dubious business activity or a recreational one – an amusement or the demands of an appetite. Facing such situations the Christian needs guidance additional to that specifically set forth in the absolute laws of Christ.

The need for principles also arises when, as sometimes happens, one Christian duty seems to conflict with another Christian duty. An example is that of a woman whose life is threatened by a pregnancy. A choice then has to be made between preserving her life and that of her unborn baby. She and her relatives might regard the killing of her unborn infant by an abortion as an act of murder, and therefore morally wrong. Medical advice would say that without an abortion she would die as would the unborn child. The duty to preserve the life of the child and the duty to save the mother seem to be in conflict with each other.

In such situations Christians have to work out a proper course of action by the adoption of biblical goals and the application of biblical principles. These entail:

i) Bringing glory to God. An absolutely basic principle is that of giving priority to actions which in their performance and in their consequences will glorify or honour the Lord – 'Whatever you eat or drink or whatever you do, do it all for the glory of God' (1 Cor. 10:31). Jesus said that man must give priority to seeking the kingdom of God and his righteousness (Matt. 6:33). This principle should always have pride of place in the Christian life and should guide us today just as much as it did the believers of Paul's day. We should always seek to discern the effect of what we propose to do on the honour of the Lord we claim to serve. Each of us must ask himself or herself, 'Will the Lord's name and his honour in the eyes of the world around me be enhanced or damaged by what I do?'

ii) Showing compassion to the needy. In a debate with Pharisees about the Sabbath, Jesus cited an Old Testament incident in which David and his men were given consecrated bread (Matt. 12:1-14). Under one of Moses' laws they ought not to have eaten this but Ahimelech, the priest of the day, gave it to them *because they were hungry* and no other bread was available (1 Sam. 21:6). Ahimelech had obeyed the law requiring love for neighbours and had given it precedence over the ceremonial law that made 'the bread of the presence' sacred to priests.

Our Lord clearly endorsed what Ahimelech did and showed that for him too the *need* of human beings in a *situation* of distress took precedence over the ceremonial law relating to 'the bread of the presence'. In applying this to plucking ears of corn on the

Sabbath, Jesus was saying that the Old Testament provision allowing travellers to satisfy their hunger by eating crops as they travelled was an expression of love for neighbours and more important than the laws sanctifying the Sabbath. The principle is strengthened by the concluding section of his discourse describing his role in the day of judgment when the sheep and the goats will be separated. And the separation will be based on whether or not those concerned have been compassionate to the needs of the least significant members of society (Matt. 25:31-46).

iii) Working for the well-being of others. While Paul insisted that he was free to eat meat that was offered for sale in a market even if it had previously been offered to an idol in a pagan temple, he also took into consideration the possible consequences of doing so (1 Cor. 8 and 10). He would think, as noticed above, of a convert from paganism, a 'weak brother', who did not yet know that an idol was a spiritual non-entity with no power to help or harm anyone. If he ate 'idol-meat', such a new convert might follow his example and by eating the meat in ignorance be drawn back into pagan sacrifice. For Paul the risk of such a consequence was too great – he would not eat meat at all! He would not allow his knowledge that the idol had no reality to be the cause of a weak brother or sister falling away from Christ (1 Cor. 8:12f).

Paul's principle was to give over-riding consideration to the need of neighbours. As a result the welfare of his weaker brother cancelled out his freedom to eat meat that had been dedicated to an idol. He then gave his readers a general principle to guide them in such matters, 'Do not cause anyone to stumble, whether Jews or Greeks or the church of God' (1 Cor. 10:32).

iv) Caring for oneself. We cannot properly keep Christ's law and meet the goals of Christian ethics if we neglect our own bodies and souls. Jesus' second greatest commandment was that we love our neighbours *as ourselves*. This puts the self on a level with neighbours. It does not exclude self-love and self-care but makes it equal with our need to love and care for others.

Paul reminds us that our bodies are the temple – the dwelling-place of the Holy Spirit – and that as the Lord's redeemed people our bodies are not our own but instruments through which we are to glorify God. The example that gave rise to this remark was that of joining the body of a believer with that of a harlot, an offence that Paul says is a sin against the body (1 Cor. 6:18-20). Clearly we are to care for and nourish our bodies and at all costs to avoid sinning against them.

At the same time Jesus put the spotlight on man's inner life. He insisted that a man's character is an expression of what comes out from his inner self, from his heart (Mark 7:14-23). The good man is one who stores up good things in his heart and the evil man is one who has filled his heart with evil things (Luke 6:45). The underlying implication, surely, is that each individual is responsible for what he admits to and stores up in his mind. This teaching echoes the words of Proverbs 4:23: 'Above all else, guard your heart, for it is the wellspring of life.' In terms of one's moral life then each individual is his or her own keeper and must set a goal of filling his or her mind with goodness and virtue. As Paul put it, 'Set your hearts on things above' (Col. 3:1).

We are morally responsible, then, to love and care for ourselves as physical, spiritual and moral beings.

v) Enjoying and granting liberty of conscience. Another biblical principle, 'liberty of conscience', comes into the picture here. This says that in matters not covered by biblical absolutes the Christian is to make his or her own decisions on the basis of biblical principles. It also requires individual Christians and their churches to grant to fellow Christians, whose decisions and actions may differ from their own, the same liberty that they themselves expect to receive.

Liberty of conscience is prominent in Romans 14 in relation to eating of animal flesh and the observance of special days (including, probably, the Sabbath). Paul asserts that those who eat meat and those who do not do so must accept and not condemn one another, because each is accepted by God and so stands or falls before the Lord (vv. 1-4). Similarly some observe days and others do not, but each does what he does 'to the Lord'. Differing or even apparently opposing behaviour patterns can, therefore, be equally acceptable to God.

The principle is that Christians, who love and serve and are responsible to the same Lord, must accept one another without passing judgment on matters that are open to differences of opinion, that is, matters that are not governed by absolute laws (Rom. 14:1). Each must accept the other as he or she has been accepted by Christ (Rom. 15:7).

It seems, then, that Christians, while ensuring that their actions do not set a bad example to others, should feel free to act as in conscience they feel is right before God, without looking over their shoulders to discover what other Christians think. Equally they are duty bound to accept as full fellow believers, people who in matters not proscribed in our Lord's absolute commands think and act differently from themselves. How different church life might be if this were the goal of all Christians!

Conclusion

The Christian is meant to live 'under law to Christ' and thus to keep the absolute laws of biblical morality – no murder, no adultery, no stealing, no false witness and no coveting of what belongs to others. He is meant to love the Lord with his whole being and to love his neighbours, as he loves himself.

Balancing the various factors can cause much heart-searching and requires that each individual give careful thought to what he or she should or should not do. Each must ensure that they know what the law of Christ requires of them and that their supreme motive is to fulfil that law and to achieve the goals set down in Scripture as appropriate to Christian goodness.

Some Christians feel 'ill-at-ease' with having to think things out for themselves. They would prefer to be told what they should or should not do. Such folk often gravitate to fringe or cultic groups that have legalistic systems and authoritarian leaders.

To weigh up and apply the relevant demands of Christ's law and the goals that express proper Christian morality demands a life of deep prayerfulness and of submissive dependence on the Holy Spirit.

4

The early Old Testament period

The records in Genesis 1–5 show that God gave the first human beings certain instructions about how they should conduct their lives. We call those instructions 'Creation Ordinances'.

Creation Ordinances

These ordinances are sometimes regarded as constituting a universal law of God, which is basic to but distinct from the later law of Moses and the still later law of Christ. They seem, however, to be more a set of guiding principles than a code of specific laws. Yet they carried something of the force of law because, as Paul says, right from creation man was in receipt of divine revelation and actually suppressed the truth by being wicked. They were without excuse because the revelation had been clear and as a result God gave them over to the sinful desires of their hearts. Clearly they failed to attain to what God expected of them – they missed the mark – and so were sinners before God (Rom. 1:19-32, cf. 2:14-15).

From the records in the first two chapters of Genesis we can say that the Creation Ordinances involved:

1. The duty to work

Man was told that he was to rule over and subdue the rest of animate creation (Gen. 1:26). This ordinance required that men work and made that activity one of their duties (Gen. 2:15). That God expected men and women to work surely invested all work with real dignity. The Fall, however changed the picture and drained away some of that dignity – man's work even in finding sustenance for himself, became 'painful toil' and was the cause of sweat on his brow (Gen. 3:18f.). Clearly this ordinance also gave man authority to use the resources of the earth for his own benefit and in particular to provide his food, though as yet the eating of animal flesh was not authorised. It did not, however, as the modern New Age Movement claims, encourage Jews and Christians into unrestrained use and abuse of the earth's resources.

2. The responsibilities of family life
Our first parents were instructed to reproduce their own kind (Gen. 1:28). Only by increasing his own population could man subdue the rest of creation. In order to achieve this goal in an orderly fashion God ordained that men and women form stable and permanent marriage relationships (Gen. 2:18-24). Men were to 'leave' their parental homes and then (after the leaving) 'cleave' to and become one flesh with their wives. Subsequent narratives show that Adam, his sons and succeeding generations established marriage relationships, which, as far as we know, were permanent. It was within these marriages that children were produced and nurtured.

3. Respect for human life
The Lord's response to Cain after he murdered Abel clearly shows this requirement – 'Your brother's blood cries out to me from the ground. Now you are under a curse and driven from the ground that opened its mouth to receive your brother's blood' (Gen. 4:10-16). Cain had acted sinfully and was punished because he had failed to respect the sanctity of his brother's life. He therefore had to leave the area where his offence had been committed but nonetheless the Lord cared for him and marked him as a sign that his life, despite his crime, was sacrosanct – 'If anyone kills Cain, he will suffer vengeance seven times over' (Gen. 4:15). This anticipates a more general provision for upholding the sanctity of life in the precepts given to Noah and in the Ten Commandments (Gen. 9:5,6; Exod. 20:13).

4. The model of rest from work on the seventh day
The story of the creation tells us that God rested from his work on the seventh day and made that day holy (Gen. 2:2). Making objects or persons holy meant setting them apart from similar things or

persons and dedicating or consecrating them to a particular purpose. Thus the vessels in the tabernacle were holy in the sense that they were reserved for use in the worship of God. In the case of the seventh day it meant making the day different from the six other days of the week and setting it apart for a special purpose or special purposes such as rest from labour and worship of the Lord.

However, despite the obvious model provided by the seventh day of the creation cycle, it must be noticed that there is no other mention of Sabbath and no reference to Sabbath observance before the time of Moses. Nonetheless some scholars think that the word, 'remember', with which the fourth commandment begins, suggests that Sabbath was kept before the decalogue was given.

Precepts given to Noah

The stories presenting the life, times and precepts given to Noah (Genesis 6–10) begin by recording very serious moral decline. The Lord saw man's great wickedness (Gen. 6:6) and responded with the Flood, which wiped out all but one family (Gen. 6:5-7,11-13). In doing so God showed that he held human beings fully responsible for their thoughts and conduct. Clearly their behaviour involved deliberate departure from standards (presumably the Creation Ordinances) of which they were aware. Indeed Paul's commentary in Romans 1:18-32 confirms that the departure from God and his standards was deliberate – men 'exchanged the truth of God for a lie, and worshipped and served created things rather than the Creator'.

The instructions given to Noah and his family after the Flood repeat and, to a considerable degree, reiterate and develop the principles and the way of life set out in the Creation Ordinances. Though they set out ideals for living and in a sense imposed obligations, they are not presented as a code of laws.

The principles/precepts given to Noah involved:

• *Reproducing the race* (Gen. 9:1, 7; 10). This precept assumes and includes marriage, which was clearly standard practice in Noah's family and in the generations that followed.

• *Ruling over creation and, in the process, engaging in work.* Noah was told that all other creatures were given into his hands, i.e., into human hands to be under human control (Gen. 9:2).

• *Eating the flesh of animals provided the blood was first drained from it* (Gen. 9:3, 4). The eating of animal flesh was a new provision at this point (the creation ordinances only mention food of a vegetable nature).

• *Respecting human life* (Gen. 9:5, 6). Because man was created in the image of God, anyone who took human life was to forfeit his own life and other human beings were given the right to exact that punishment – 'by man shall his blood be shed'. Though not stated as a law, this precept clearly carried a strong sanction and the ultimate penalty for those who flouted it.

• *Respecting parents* (Gen. 9:21-27). Even those who, like Noah under the influence of alcohol, acted foolishly were to be treated properly.

The practice of the patriarchs

The story of the patriarchs, Abraham, Isaac, Jacob and his twelve sons is told in Genesis 12 to 50. These chapters bring Bible history into a recognisable time frame involving roughly the nineteenth and eighteenth centuries BC, i.e., from around 1900 to 1700 BC.

In these records we still find no formal code of moral law and no evidence of God bestowing further revelation of ethical values. However the lives of their various heroes show that they had moral values that in many ways anticipated the obligations that were later imposed in quite specific terms through the Ten Commandments. Sometimes these obligations were observed nobly and sometimes they were ignobly defied.

Sabbath is still a missing element but the absence of any mention of it is not proof that it was not known or observed by some or all of the patriarchs.

1. Noble actions

Abraham's departure from Ur of the Chaldees to go to a land that he didn't know was an act of faith and obedience to God. His determination to obey what God required showed itself on numerous occasions during the rest of his life, but on none more conspicuously than when he took his especially precious son, Isaac, to Mount Moriah in full readiness to offer him as a sacrifice to the Lord (Gen. 22).

Abraham and his nephew Lot found it necessary to separate because their herdsmen were squabbling over a limited supply of pasture (Gen. 13). He allowed Lot to choose where he would settle and said that if Lot went in one direction he would go in another. Lot chose the well-watered Jordan valley and set up camp near the town of Sodom. Abraham went south to the Hebron area, which was likely to be less fertile. While Lot appears to be self-centred and covetous of what would be to his greatest advantage, Abraham is presented as mild, self-effacing, peace-loving and ready to accept a situation that might be less advantageous to his own interests.

Respect for life showed itself in the actions taken by Reuben and Judah to save Joseph from death (Gen. 37:21-27). Respect for life was joined with respect for parents when Joseph, then in high office in Egypt, was approached by his brothers for food. He showed a deep concern for the well-being and for the survival of his father Jacob and his younger brother Benjamin (Gen. 42-47).

Marriage and its permanence are seen in the fidelity of Abraham to Sarah (even if additional wives and concubines were also part of his family). After Sarah's death, Abraham being old wanted a wife for his son Isaac and, in order to avoid taking a Canaanite, sent to Mesopotamia where Rebekah was found. When she arrived Isaac brought her into his mother's tent and in some formal way married her – 'she became his wife' (Gen. 24:67).

Clearly Jacob also had a formal marriage ceremony, when in Laban's home friends and neighbours – 'all the people of the place' – were called together for a feast after which Leah was given to Jacob (Gen. 29:22, 23). The sexual relationship followed, providing an illustration of the knowledge that the intimacies and the cleaving of marriage are meant to be reserved till *after* the leaving from parental guardianship and *after* formal marriage. A week later Jacob was given Rachel, who had, of course, been the bride he preferred. When in due course she died in childbirth he marked her burial place with a memorial pillar, which surely indicated that there had been a continuing, a permanent and an affectionate bond between them (Gen. 35:18-20).

Joseph's rejection of the seductive advances of Potiphar's wife indicates that he was well aware of the sanctity of marriage and of the sinfulness of violating its bond. 'How,' he asked, 'could I do such a wicked thing and sin against God?' (Gen. 39:9). Clearly in his mind there was a standard of behaviour to which he was required to adhere. Joseph's concern for truthfulness and complete integrity on the part of his brothers (Gen. 42:14-17) is surely indicative of a standard that must have governed his own life.

2. Ignoble actions

The records of the Patriarchs also indicate lapses even from the greatest heroes. The descriptions of their misdemeanours are essentially factual. While mostly, however, they don't spell out moral condemnation, they do tend to imply some abhorrence of practices later proscribed in the law of Moses. These include:

- *Sexual licence*. This is illustrated by the situation involving intended homosexual rape that arose when Lot and his family were in Sodom (Gen. 19:1-11). It also emerges in the incestuous actions of his two daughters after they settled in a new location in the hill country (the mountains, Gen. 19: 30-38).

  The sexual liaison between Judah and his widowed daughter-in-law (Gen. 38) is another instance of sexual immorality. Tamar tricked him into this because his son Onan had refused to fulfil the *levirate* custom of producing offspring for his deceased brother Er, and because, after Onan died, a marriage that had been promised her with his younger son, Shelah, had not been arranged.

  In Latin, the word *levir* means 'brother-in-law and our phrase *levirate marriage* focuses on a relationship between a widow and her brother-in-law, in which he is the biological but not the legal father of her child. That Onan's failure is said to have been wicked in the Lord's sight' indicates that at that stage in the history of revelation there was divine approval of the practice of a deceased husband's brother (i.e. his widow's brother-in-law or *levir*) fathering a child or children on his behalf. However, while *levirate marriage* is accepted and endorsed in the story, harlotry (in which Judah deliberately participated) and incestuous encounters between kith and kin (such as occurred between Judah and Tamar) are not.

- *Kidnap*. Joseph's brothers were guilty of this when they sold him into slavery (Gen. 37:12-36)

- *Dishonesty*. Jacob was dishonest when he stole Esau's birthright (Gen. 27:1-40). So was Abraham who deceived both Pharaoh and Abimelech about the status of his wife (Gen. 12:10-19; 20:1-18). Isaac treated Abimelech in the same way (Gen. 26:1-11).

- *Covetousness*. Though not specifically mentioned, this was obviously at the root of Lot's decision to go to Sodom (Gen. 13:1-13) and of many of the offences that are recorded in these patriarchal narratives.

What emerges clearly is that, before the Ten Commandments were given through Moses, there was, despite the absence of a promulgated code of moral law, an awareness of moral obligation. Men of the patriarchal era, like those of earlier times, knew that certain forms of behaviour were expected of them. The principles made evident at creation and through the precepts given to Noah were somehow made plain to a godless world by God himself (Rom. 1:19). They were written on men's hearts and consciences to a degree sufficient to leave them, as Paul put it, 'without excuse' (Rom. 1:20). At the same time the fact that Gentiles, who did not have the law of Moses, did by nature what that law required shows that the requirements of divine law were and, indeed, still are written on men's hearts.

Conclusion

It is clear that before Moses there was knowledge of God's moral requirements, that by itself this was not sufficient to change the hearts and lives of sinful men. Yet for men outside God's covenant relationship it was, and for the unbeliever today it still is, enough to leave them without excuse.

The widespread incidence in this early period of what the Bible calls sin is vividly shown not just in Genesis, but also in Paul's description of the moral decline of the human race (Rom. 1:18-30): 'For since the creation of the world God's invisible qualities – his eternal power and divine nature – have been clearly seen, being understood from what has been made, so that men are without excuse' (v.20).

It was this incidence of sin, which, according to Galatians 3:19, made the introduction of a code of law essential. As Paul puts it, the law given to Moses at Sinai *was added because of transgressions* until the Seed to whom the promise referred had come. That 'seed', as verse 16 of the same chapter affirms, means the 'one person', who is Christ. The role of the Mosaic Law was that of an interim provision for the period between Moses and Christ.

5

The first five commandments

It is convenient and, hopefully, helpful to divide our consideration of the Ten Commandments into two halves. In doing so we must, of course, remember that they belong together and should always be treated as one body of divine instruction.

1. You shall have no other gods before me

This commandment is concerned with the object of man's worship, with the one *whom* he worships. It requires an exclusive relationship with God, who allows no rivals and no multiple loyalties, no other god in addition to or instead of himself – literally 'no other god before my face.'

In making this demand the commandment also excludes the fertility rituals and occult practices which were always prominent in the religion of the nations around Israel. These purported to stimulate fertility by magic. The ancestors of Israel had, in fact, come from Mesopotamia (Ur of the Chaldees, Gen. 11:28) and the religions of that area and of Egypt, where they themselves had been enslaved, seem to have retained an attraction for many Israelites. At the time of the conquest of Caanan Joshua had to appeal to them to choose between those gods and God the Lord (Josh. 24:14ff).

In subsequent centuries Baal worship, which included these evils, was a constant snare to the Israelites, many of whom tried to combine it with worship of the Lord. It seems that they wanted to keep, or perhaps we should say they felt they had to keep, on the right side of the gods that were thought to own the land they had occupied!

Towards the end of the seventh century BC, when the threat of exile hung heavily over Judah, the only surviving part of ancient Israel, Zephaniah's prophecy indicated that Baal worship was still in vogue. The Lord said:

... hand against Judah and against all who live in
... cut off from this place every remnant of Baal ...

Su... ...ious syncretism (putting together systems that differ in
essen... ...l content and meaning) was absolutely forbidden by this
commandment.

Babylonian and Caananite fertility religions considered it
necessary for male gods to have female consorts. Hence the stone
and the pole, the *mazzebah* and the *asherah* symbols of the Baal
and his consort at the Caananite shrines known as 'high places'.
Hence too the cultic prostitution in the supposed interests of fertility
that took place at those shrines. The Lord, as the author of life,
needed no such consort and his people needed no fertility rituals
or occultic alternatives to worshipping him. He says,

> I am the LORD; that is my name!
>> I will not give my glory to another
>> or my praise to idols (Isa. 42:8)

The first commandment also had political implications because
in Old Testament times a nation and its deity were thought to be
so closely linked that victory or defeat for the nation was seen as
victory or defeat for its god. Thus, when the Philistines defeated
Israel and captured the Ark, which they thought was a
representation of the Lord (1 Sam. 4:7), they believed that the
LORD had also been defeated. To symbolise this they placed the
Ark in their temple beside or before an image of their god, Dagon.
But during the night the Lord reversed the picture and the statue
representing Dagon lay in pieces before the Ark (1 Sam. 5:1-5).
Israel may have been defeated in battle but the Lord was not
defeated! God's relationship with his people was not tied to victory
or defeat in war or to the ups and downs of life in general. He
remained the sovereign Lord and was in control of all that was
happening to his creatures on earth. He is the only true God and
he is sovereign over our lives also.

What does this mean for us today? We need to think of and ask
questions about:

• *our materialism* – do we worship and value our possessions more than the Lord? Jesus said, 'You cannot serve God and money' (Luke 16:13).

• *our love of pleasure* – do we put pleasure in the place of God?

• *our hero-worship* – are we idolising politicians, entertainers, sports personalities or even friends? Are any human beings more important to us than the Lord?

The commandment demands whole-hearted devotion – 'You shall love the Lord your God with all your heart ...' But do we do so?

2. You shall not make for yourself an idol (a graven image) in the form of anything in heaven above or in the earth beneath or in the waters below. You shall not bow down to them or worship them ...

The second commandment is concerned with *how* men worship God. It outlawed all images made to represent the Lord and it prohibited Israelites from bowing down to worship such representations of their own or any other deity. The incident of the golden calf (or bull) image recorded in Exodus 32 shows how necessary it was. Aaron made the image and the people were told, 'these are your gods (or this is your God) O Israel, who brought you up out of the Land of Egypt.' Clearly it was an image that in their minds represented Jehovah/Yahweh.

The command asserts divine spirituality saying, in effect, 'God is Spirit'. Worship of the Lord must, therefore, be spiritual and not just a matter of aesthetic responses to the beauty of works of art which man himself has made (cf. Isa. 40:18-24).

The commandment forces us to ensure that our worship of God is not a mere outward form but a positive and real exercise of our spirits.

A threat was added to this commandment. It says:

For I, the LORD your God, am a jealous God, punishing the children for the sin of the fathers to the third and fourth generation of those

who hate me, but showing love to thousands who love me and keep
my commandments (Exod. 20:5,6).

This threat affirming that God would punish children to the third
and fourth generations is often regarded as a major moral problem,
but it is not as serious as some insist. There were often, it seems,
three or four generations residing in a household and the
punishment was therefore restricted to them as happened in the
case of Achan (Josh. 7:24f). It is possible or rather probable that
the emphasis is on the contrast between God's wrath extending to
(just) four generations at most and his mercies going on for ever –
to the thousandth generation of those who love him. The Hebrew
numeral could mean either thousands or thousandth and in the
International Bible Society edition of the NIV the rendering is 'to
the thousandth [generation] of those who love me'.

Throughout their history Jews have tended to regard the second
commandment as outlawing every kind of image. They, therefore,
have had no paintings at all in their synagogues.

The second commandment also raises questions for us today.
We must ask, for example,

• Is it right to have images or pictures representing the divine
persons, the Father, the Son and the Holy Spirit in our churches?

• Is it good to have drawings or paintings representing Christ
in books for our children?

• Is it right for actors to play a part in which they act or speak
as or for a divine person and so become a kind of image of that
person?

3. You shall not misuse (take in vain) the name of the LORD your God

This commandment assumes that Israel knew God's name. It
was YHWH or JHVH and had been disclosed to Moses at the
burning bush (Exod. 3:13-14). It was by this name that the Lord
identified himself when he introduced the Decalogue (Exod. 20:2).
Since vowels were not written in ancient Hebrew the exact form

and pronunciation of this sacred name are not known. In addition it was never spoken for fear of breaching this third commandment. All we know is that the first Hebrew letter, 'Yodh', can be a 'J' or a 'Y' in our alphabet and the third, 'Waw', can be 'W' or 'V'. The sacred name could, then, be Yahweh, Yahveh, Jahweh or Jehovah.

In the ancient world the disclosure of a personal name was always an indication of friendship and of commitment to the person privileged to receive the disclosure. Thus when two chieftains made a treaty each disclosed his secret personal name to the other as an indication of genuine commitment to him. Similarly the fact that the Israelites knew God's name was evidence that he had entered into a special relationship with them. He had committed himself to them and they were his covenant people.

In the succeeding Mosaic literature it becomes clear that there were at least three ways in which the Israelites could legitimately use God's name.

• *As a mark of identity.* They were his people called by his name and were to be known as such (Deut. 28:10).

• *As a focus for worship.* The Lord promised to put his name at a site where they would worship him (Deut.12:4-7).

• *As a way of affirming oaths.* The Israelites were permitted to affirm the truth by using the Lord's name as they made oaths. (Deut. 10:20, cf. 6:13).

The commandment forbids misuse or abuse of the Lord's name – i.e., its use for a false purpose (one inconsistent with his character). It is not to be used in a vain or empty way, i.e., without the solemn purposes (above), which the Lord himself had prescribed. This meant not using his name,

• *in conjunction with conduct which profaned it* (cf. Amos 2:6-8; Ezek. 36:20f.).

• *in an attempt to obtain personal gain.* An example would be its use as a charm or as part of a charm, with the aim of gaining some benefit for oneself or for someone else. Simon Magus had such an aim (Acts 8:9-21). To this day 'simony' is the attempt to purchase position or spiritual power in church life. The sons of Sceva (Acts 19:13-16) had a similar aim when they illegitimately used the name of Jesus and got themselves into trouble for doing so.

• *to perjure oneself.* Perjury is false witness under an oath – in Israel an oath that used the Lord's name. 'Do not swear falsely by my name and so profane the name of your God. I am the Lord' (Lev. 19:12). Our Lord's rejection of insincere or artificial oaths and his insistence that 'Yes' mean 'Yes' and 'No' mean 'No' (Matt. 5:33-36) arise from and echo this commandment. His followers are to be men and women of integrity, whose word can always be regarded as completely true and totally reliable.

This commandment, like the second, ends with a threat – 'the Lord will not hold anyone guiltless who misuses his name.' The threat relates to abuses that involved or could involve a paganising of an Israelite's theology and religion. The Lord would not ignore such misuse of his name.

This commandment also speaks to us today. It causes us to examine ourselves in relation to,

- *Our integrity.* If we have been baptised into Christ's name, we are in a very real sense using his name to identify ourselves as those who belong to him. Any lack of proper Christian conduct profanes that name. If we have done so, or are doing so now, we must put matters right by coming before him in true repentance.

- *Our worship.* We can use the Lord's name emptily and without any real devotion of heart. We can also try to make it a password to gain something for ourselves. If this is the case we must change our ways.

- *Our oaths.* Many people either directly or indirectly misuse and profane the Lord's name in affirmations or expletives. If we are guilty we must repent and change our ways. In addition we must be men and women of absolute truthfulness – our 'Yes' must mean 'Yes' and our 'No' must mean 'No' (Matt. 5:37).

4. Remember the Sabbath day by keeping it holy. Six days you shall labour and do all your work ...

It was noticed earlier that there is no record of Sabbath obligation or observance before the time of Moses. Genesis 2:2 tells us what God did after he finished his work of creation and not what his creatures did or were commanded to do.

The first reference to the observance of the Sabbath is in connection with the collection of manna in the wilderness after the Exodus (Exod. 16:23-30). It reads as if a new obligation was being imposed in conjunction with the provision of the manna but, as noted earlier, some think that the word 'Remember' with which the command begins indicates recall to what had obtained earlier. Actually much later, in the fifth century BC, Ezra said that the Sabbath had been given at Sinai (Neh. 9:13-14).

The Hebrew word 'Sabbath' has the force of 'making an end' or of 'ceasing from something'. The Sabbath was thus a day of ceasing from one's normal toil and labour; it was a day of rest. It was not, however, a day of total inactivity. Wives were not among those to whom it was applied, an indication, probably, that domestic duties essential to family life were not forbidden. In Leviticus 23:3 we learn that it was also designated as a day of solemn assembly, obviously envisaging some kind of religious activity the nature of which is not specified.

The command has a reverse as well as an obverse side. This is that in providing one day of rest after six days of work it endorsed the 'creation ordinance' and indicated that man was meant to be a worker. It showed not just that God was providing a day of rest each week but that he continued to expect his creatures to engage in work.

The command operates in two directions, the godward (a Sabbath to the Lord your God) which seems to be the primary thrust, and the manward (rest for you yourself, your offspring, your servants etc.). By moving into the manward dimension the command introduces an element of what we now call human rights – family and servants were given the right to have a day of rest from labour after six days of work.

At Sinai the command was based on the example set by God who rested from his work of creation on the seventh day (Ex. 20:11). However, when Moses formally proclaimed the commandments for a second time just before Israel entered the promised land, the Sabbath was presented as a remembrance of the redemption of the Israelites from the slavery of Egypt – 'Remember that you were slaves in Egypt and that the LORD your God brought you out of there with a mighty hand …' (Deut. 5:15).

It is important to realise that the provision of one day of rest after every six days of work was not just a memorial of creation and redemption but an expression of God's concern for the welfare of his people. It was a provision that mitigated to some degree the effects of the Fall, which had turned work into toil (Gen. 3:19). Here was gracious relief from that toil.

When the Jews were in exile in Babylon in the sixth century BC, they were unable to maintain their temple worship or their great pilgrimage feasts at Jerusalem, Sabbath observance was possible and became, in fact, one of two distinguishing marks of a Jew. Ezekiel even announced that God had given the Sabbath as a sign of the covenant relation between himself and his people. It assured them that they were still holy (or set apart for him) and that he had not forsaken them (Ezek. 20:12). The other mark of national identity was the circumcision of male infants.

It is also important that though Jesus did not specifically quote the fourth commandment he clearly endorsed the principle of one day's rest after six days of work. 'The Sabbath,' he said, 'was made for man' (Mark 2:27). He was saying that, in the mind and purpose of the Creator, men need such a day of rest and that, in his grace and for man's sake (i.e., for our benefit), he ordained it.

The question of how the fourth commandment is to be applied by Christians today needs detailed examination in the light of the fuller revelation we have in the New Testament. What is clear is that man needs a day of rest from the work by which he earns his living. The New Testament put the first day of the week, the

'Lord's Day', in place of the old Sabbath, but the principle of a day that is different, a day for rest and for worship, remains. People need it and because of this God graciously ordained it. We Christians must be careful to preserve it as the Lord's day.

5. Honour your father and your mother so that you may live long in the land the LORD your God is giving you

This commandment brings manward relationships into the primary position – it is concerned with the welfare of human parents. However, the fact that we receive life through our parents puts them in a mediating role between us and God, the giver of life, and, because of this, honour for parents can be seen as something which projects itself beyond them to God. This commandment thus retains an element of a godward dimension as well as a manward one.

The fact that the manward dimension is primary brings into focus again the 'human rights' aspect of the Decalogue – parents have a right to the respect, the support, the love and even the obedience of their offspring. (The Hebrew word translated 'honour' implies not only an acknowledgement of another person's dignity but actual submission to that person's authority.)

The command also safeguards the 'authority-structure' needed for well-ordered family life by affirming that respect is due to both parents. This puts mothers on a level with fathers not only in terms of respect but also of rights and, in some measure at least, of authority within the family. Civil law supported this by making injury caused to a parent, and any act of cursing a parent, capital offences (See Exod. 21:15,17, cf. Lev. 20:9; Deut. 21:18-21; 27:16). An injury caused to a parent was, in fact, a more serious offence than one caused to other persons. Compare, for example, the capital punishment prescribed in Exodus 21:15 and 17 with the lesser penalties for other crimes in the verses that follow.

While both parents had responsibilities for educating their children (Prov. 1:8; 6:20), a father had a sacred duty to teach religious truths to his sons (Exod. 12:26,27; 13:8; Deut. 4:9). It is even thought by some that a major purpose behind the fifth commandment was to preserve within the family the true faith of

God's people since any repudiation of parents would be, or could be, at the same time a repudiation of that faith.

This command has appended to it a statement promising those who are obedient long life in the land God was about to give to the Israelites. This promise could be understood as providing a motivating purpose for honouring parents or as indicating the result of obeying the command. In Deuteronomy 5:16 the additional promise that those who obeyed it would benefit in the land certainly points to obedience bringing benefits.

These promises create difficulties for some people because good sons or daughters do not always enjoy long life while some of the wicked do. Their worry may, however, result from a misunderstanding of the purpose of the threat. Its focus seems to have been on the thought that Israel *as a nation* would remain in and prosper in the land and *not* on a blanket promise of longevity to those individuals who faithfully honour their parents. By implication God was saying that the nation's tenure of the land would depend heavily on the stability of family life which obedience to this command would produce.

The fifth commandment speaks to us today by presenting us with solemn duties:

• *to respect or honour in the fullest possible way those through whom life came to us*

• *to care for frail or poverty-stricken elderly parents*

• *to honour difficult parents even if they are wicked, apostate, unbelieving or antagonistic to ourselves.*

Fulfilling these requirements, and especially the last one, can sometimes be difficult. Whatever the difficulties, we Christians must try to live by the principles of the Christian ethic as displayed in the New Testament (the law of Christ). That sometimes means going not just an extra mile but extra miles in expressing respect and love for those who make themselves unlovely and who in our eyes may even be unlovable. We need the mind of Christ who, 'while we were still sinners' (or still antagonistic towards God) 'died for us' (Rom. 5:8).

6

The second five commandments

The second five commandments focus particularly on our obligations towards our fellow human beings. However, as we noticed earlier, because these are commands given by God, those who break them are guilty also of sinning against him.

6. You shall not murder

The Hebrew verb in this command is used exclusively of killing human beings and does not relate to the slaughter of animals. In the NIV it is translated 'do not murder' rather than 'do not kill' which is found in both the AV and the RSV. However, its meaning is rather wider than murder and can include acts of manslaughter and probably also of suicide. A translation like, 'you shall not take human life' or 'you shall not commit homicide' would seem to be appropriate.

The command did not, however, prohibit all killing of human beings because the Israelites were permitted, and in some cases were required, to kill enemies in war (e.g. 1 Sam. 15:3). They also had civil laws, which prescribed execution as the penalty for murder and for other crimes such as cursing parents, adultery, sexual perversion and blasphemy (Lev. 20:10ff; 24:16).

Nonetheless this commandment declares that life is sacred and that, unless a person forfeited the right to life by virtue of some criminal offence, he was to be allowed to live out his natural life. It further imposed on every individual a positive responsibility to make this possible by abstaining from the killing of human beings.

Subsidiary legislation also required that an Israelite should not put another person's life at risk by being careless. Thus, for example, anyone building a new house with a flat roof had to build a parapet lest someone should fall off, in which case the owner would become guilty of bloodshed (Deut. 22:8). In effect each man was made to be his brother's keeper and each individual was given the most basic of all human rights, the 'right to live'. Thus human life is indeed declared to be sacred and, as far as individuals motivated by hatred and even with cause for revenge are concerned, absolutely inviolable.

While the responsibility to respect and preserve human life is clear and carelessness must be avoided there is a great difference between accidental and deliberate killings. Israelite law recognised this by providing 'cities of refuge' as safe havens for the protection of non-intentional killers. Similarly anyone killing a person caught in the act of burglary was not a murderer, but if he killed the intruder later (i.e., premeditatedly) he would have been guilty of that crime (Exod. 22:2-3).

The sixth commandment reminds us that in God's eyes every human life is sacred and that no individual ever has the right to kill another person. Murder is always a most serious offence before God.

The command speaks to us about issues of importance in our own day.

• *about war, capital punishment, abortion, euthanasia, etc*. In each of these a human life is taken.

• *about the carelessness which can cause an accidental death*. Accidents take place in homes, on the roads, on farms or in industry. The commandment demands that we strive our utmost to protect other lives ensuring, for example, that electrical items are safe, that nothing hot be allowed to spill on and burn children or adults, that our cars are mechanically safe with effective brakes, etc.

7. You shall not commit adultery
Adultery is usually defined as sexual union between a married person and someone who is not his or her legal spouse. Behind our English word is the Latin verb *adulterare,* meaning 'to pollute', 'to debase', or 'to falsify'. Union with a partner other than the one to whom one is married pollutes or 'adulterates' a relationship that has been ordained to be sacred and exclusive.

In the Sermon on the Mount Jesus made it clear that the intrusion of any sexual attraction into the thoughts of a married person is adulterous even if no physical union occurs (Matt. 5:28). When David looked lustfully at Bathsheba, he had already committed adultery even before he sent a messenger to bring her to him (2 Sam. 11:1-6).

The command, like others of manward application, also conferred 'rights'. A husband is given the right to a stable marriage, in which his wife did not become involved with another man. The wife had the right to be the possession of one man rather than the plaything of many. Their children with their mother had the right to a stable home. As far as we know the wife, though protected in many ways, did not at this stage have the absolute right to the sole possession of her husband.

While men were discouraged from marrying many wives (Deut. 17:17), they were not prevented by law from having more than one. The Creation Ordinance and the New Testament indicate clearly, however, that God's intention always was and is that one man and one woman should be faithful to each other as long as each remains alive.

The sanctity of marriage was further safeguarded by a considerable number of laws prohibiting relationships that would undermine it. These included incest, homosexual acts, bestiality and harlotry (Lev. 19:29; 20:10-21). There were regulations dealing with the raping of a virgin girl and requiring the offending man to marry his victim and to lose the right ever to divorce her, which also point to and strengthen the sanctity of marriage (Deut. 22:29). In the divine intention to effect a sexual union is to enter a lifelong commitment, a one-flesh union (Gen. 2:24).

This commandment has much to say to us today:

• *about maintaining the integrity of marriage*. It challenges the permissiveness in sexual relationships which is character-istic of much modern society. It demands that Christians main-tain the biblical standard for marriage, that is, one man and one woman united in love and for life.

• *about maintaining the purity of our inward thoughts.* Our Lord, as we noticed above, said that adultery is not just a matter of physical sexual union but of inward thoughts and desires. A look that expresses lust is a form, an inward form, of adultery (Matt. 5:28). An emotional association that intrudes into a marriage and damages the husband-wife relationship may not involve physical sexual union but it is still adultery. It adulterates or, at least, is in serious danger of adulterating the marriage. Christians must ever keep Jesus' words before them and avoid having lustful thoughts and emotional entanglement with persons of the opposite sex to whom they are not properly married.

8. You shall not steal

At first sight this commandment seems simply to proscribe the theft of anything belonging to someone else. In doing so it would affirm the right of an individual to own property and to retain it as his or her own.

There is, however, some difficulty in that the tenth commandment, which says 'You shall not covet...' also affirms the right to hold property by prohibiting the covetous desires that produce theft. This apparent overlap seems somewhat strange in a list of just five commandments (6-10) designed to control inter-personal human relations.

Some scholars feel that the eighth commandment was given to outlaw kidnap – the stealing of a person. They point out that in Exodus 21:16 and Deuteronomy 24:7 the same Hebrew verb (*ganab*, to steal) is used for that offence which, like murder and adultery, carried the death penalty. Thus understood the commandment fits in as part of a group of three, for the breach of which the same civil penalty (death) was due. All three are seen, in fact, as protecting the integrity of the human person by conferring on him the right to life, to a stable marriage and to freedom. If this is correct the eighth command confers not the 'right to property' but the 'right to freedom'. In that event the right to property is still safeguarded by the tenth commandment.

Taking the commandment as referring to kidnap is attractive

in many ways, but references to it in the rest of the Bible mostly relate it not to kidnap but to stealing in a more general sense. The Septuagint, a Greek version of the Old Testament produced before our Lord's time, used *klepto,* the ordinary Greek word for stealing, and the New Testament also does so. At the same time most New Testament references to the tenth commandment emphasise not so much stealing as the covetous desires which might lead to it. It seems better therefore to take the eighth commandment in the traditionally accepted sense of forbidding all theft. In doing so we recognise that, if the original intention related to kidnap, the command was subsequently extended to include all stealing. In that event we have to regard the command as conferring both the right to personal freedom and the right to own and to hold property.

Again there are important applications to ourselves today:

• *in relation to having what rightfully belongs to others.* We might have items which have not been paid for or that have been borrowed and not returned. Gaining employment, promotion, privilege or prestige through bribery or other doubtful means is, in fact, stealing what by right belongs to another.

• *in relation to depriving others of their liberty.* In recent years kidnap and the selling of those abducted into slavery has been rife in some countries. In many places people suffer from an economic slavery that dominates their lives. Sometimes possessive parents selfishly deprive their offspring of freedom to be themselves or to realise their ambitions and find fulfilment in a different path of life, for example, in marriage.

• *in relation to our stewardship before God.* We can rob him of our company by failing to worship him and of our money by failing to give it in offerings etc. And if we are guilty, as surely we all are, we must try to put things right. Note Malachi 3:6-12.

9. You shall not give false testimony against your neighbour

This commandment is primarily concerned with testimony given at court whether one is making a charge against someone else or defending oneself against a charge.

The Hebrew of Exodus 20:16 is literally, 'you shall not answer your neighbour as a lying witness.' It puts the focus on deliberate deceit. The wording in Deuteronomy 5:20 is somewhat different – 'You shall not answer your neighbour as a witness of emptiness' – and highlights legal testimony which has no basis in fact and which is, therefore, equally false. In both versions what was primarily in view was a testimony which would destroy or attempt to destroy another person's reputation by having him or her pronounced guilty of an offence he or she had not committed.

Among the laws immediately following the ten commandments, several expanded the implications of the ninth. In the first, gossip of the kind that spreads false reports, and helps someone else establish a malicious charge against an innocent person was forbidden (Exod. 23:1). In the second there was a prohibition on siding with the crowd in the context of an accusation at a court of law (Exod. 23:2). A crowd is, of course, easily whipped up to a frenzy of hate that can quickly deprive its victim(s) of any real justice. Thirdly, and perhaps surprisingly, favouritism was not to be shown to a poor man in his lawsuit (Exod. 23:3). Sympathy for such could, of course, pervert justice. But equally the poor were not to be denied justice (v.6). The effect of these laws was that the Israelite was to have nothing to do with false charges, which could have led to the punishment and, in many cases, even to the execution of a person who had been falsely accused.

In between these provisions there is a fine illustration of how justice is to work between neighbours even when they are at enmity with one another. If one found a straying animal that belonged to the other he was to bring it back to its owner. If he found an animal that had fallen because of an over-heavy load he was to help it. Justice thus combined with love for every neighbour and demanded such actions even to an enemy!

The ninth commandment was, then, primarily concerned to

ensure that every citizen of Israel enjoyed an inalienable right to legal justice. The commandment's commitment to justice was strengthened by three subsidiary laws that specified methods of securing it.

• An accusation was to be established only on the testimony of two or more witnesses (Num. 35:30; Deut. 17:6; 19:15).

• Anyone who had information relevant to a case being heard in public (Hebrew suggests being heard 'on oath') and did not disclose that information, would be held responsible for his iniquity (Lev. 5:1). Thus there was no right to silence in ancient Israel.

• A malicious witness was to receive the penalty which would have been meted out to the person he had accused if his accusation had been proved to be true (Deut. 19:16-18).

In subsequent Israelite life justice was often conspicuous by its absence – it was negated by bribery, which gave it to those who were prepared to pay for it rather than to those who were entitled to it. Samuel's sons, we read, 'took bribes and perverted justice' (1 Sam. 8:3). The prophets constantly inveighed against the injustices of those to whom they spoke. Isaiah wrote:

Your lips have spoken lies,
    and your tongue mutters wicked things.
No-one calls for justice;
    no-one pleads his case with integrity.
They rely on empty arguments and speak lies ...
    justice is far from us ...
    justice is driven back (Isa.59:3-4, 9, 14).

Through Amos, the Lord addressed the Israelites as, those who 'turn justice into bitterness,' who 'oppress the righteous and take bribes' and who 'deprive the poor of justice in the courts' (Amos 5:7,12). The penalty was to be exile in a foreign land but there was still a call for this state of affairs to be changed – 'Let justice roll on like a river, righteousness like a never-failing stream' (Amos 5:24).

At the same time the prophets and sages of the Old Testament used this ninth commandment much more broadly to outlaw every kind of falsehood. Truth is extolled and dishonesty is condemned – 'A truthful witness gives honest testimony, but a false witness tells lies … Truthful lips endure for ever, but a lying tongue lasts only a moment' (Prov. 12:17,19). The wise sage urged his son that he should 'buy the truth' and not sell it (Prov. 23:23).

The Lord Jesus came into our world as one who was 'full of grace and truth' (John 1:14, 17). He insisted that he spoke the truth (John 8:40, 45, 46). Paul made a similar claim for his own testimony before Agrippa – 'what I am saying is true' (Acts 26:25). He was concerned that his readers in Ephesus would speak 'the truth in love' (Eph. 4:15).

The ninth commandment then, like the others, speaks clearly to us today. Truthfulness and integrity are qualities to which God ever calls his people.

- *in relation to giving testimony in court.* If we are called to give such testimony we must do so with complete integrity.

- *in relation to everyday conversation.* Because it is so easy to destroy another person's reputation by malicious or even just idle gossip, we must always be concerned for the good of our neighbours and be absolutely just in what we say about them.

10. You shall not covet your neighbour's house ... or anything that belongs to your neighbour

There are slight differences between the version of this commandment found in Exodus and that in Deuteronomy. In Exodus 20:17 the first prohibition is concerned with coveting a neighbour's house while in Deuteronomy his wife comes first. Some scholars have thought that the word 'house' in the Exodus version means a 'household' and so would include a man's wife, his whole family, and possibly even his servants. Such a suggestion is unnecessary since the very next prohibition relates to wives. It is, nonetheless, possible that the Deuteronomy version reflects further progress in revelation and indicates an improvement in the status of women.

A second difference is that Deuteronomy 5:21 adds a neighbour's 'field' to the list of items not to be coveted. This reflects the fact that when Moses proclaimed the law for a second time Israel was about to settle into the land of Caanan where the ownership of land would become a reality.

This commandment strikes at the desires of the human heart and at the motivation behind wrongful action. It strengthens the prohibitions and the rights enshrined in the 6th, 7th, 8th and 9th commandments by prohibiting the thoughts that produce actions that break those commandments. Illegitimate gain, whether as a matter of desire or of activity, is proscribed. The selfishness that would deprive another of life or freedom, that would violate his marriage or rob him of property or of justice, was to have no place in Israelite life.

We find the emphasis of this commandment often reiterated in the rest of the Old Testament and in the teachings of Jesus and the apostles. It is at the very heart of Biblical morality. As Paul puts it, 'covetousness' (NIV 'greed') is idolatry' (Col. 3:5). The tenth commandment thus attacks the source of all sin, namely the desires we have in our innermost beings. It is the command that most deeply convinced the apostle Paul that he was a sinner. He says, 'I would not have known what it was to covet if the law had not said, "Do not covet"' (Rom. 7:7).

This commandment also speaks and speaks powerfully today:

• *in relation to selfish desires.* We can have desires for money or possessions, for position or power in a social group like a church or a workplace. If we are covetous of others in any way at all, we need a radical change of heart and an ability to be content with what we have.

• *in relation to things sexual.* Jesus spoke of the sinfulness of a man looking lustfully or covetously at a woman. The Book of Proverbs is filled with warnings against enticements to adultery. And nowadays, with the growth and openness of

homosexuality, we have to avoid covetousness in relation to
our own sex. If one looks at another person with lust in his or
her heart an inward change is necessary. He (or she) must ask
the Lord to cleanse his (or her) thoughts and to forgive his (or
her) sins (Ps. 51:10; Isa. 55:7). Not only so but one must
deliberately orientate himself or herself away from and against
the illicit attraction. Paul knew what he was talking about when
he said, 'Flee from sexual immorality' (1 Cor. 6:18). Purity
demands that we put distance, physical and psychological
distance between ourselves and anyone (other than our spouse)
to whom we find ourselves sexually attracted.

Moral failure after Moses' time

After the death of Joshua, spiritual and moral behaviour rapidly
deteriorated in Israel (Judg. 2:6-23). From time to time the LORD
had to chastise his people by subjecting them to attacks from their
neighbours. He raised up a succession of judges to deliver them
from their enemies (v.16) but when this happened they soon turned
back to worship other gods (v.17). The period is, therefore,
characterised as one of lawlessness when everyone did whatever
he himself wanted to do (Judg. 17:6).

Some of the stories in Judges, like the burning of a thousand
people in the tower of Shechem and the apparent killing of
Jephthah's daughter, are quite horrific and can be an
embarrassment to Christians. Samson acting with arrogant
irresponsibility is another example (14:1-20; 16:1; 16:4-22). The
usual explanation of these happenings is that in the overall context
of revelation there were periods of advance and times of regression.
Periods like that of the Judges bear witness to man's frailty and to
his need of a Saviour who could effect a perfect and an eternal
redemption.

During the monarchy, moral failure continued to show man's
great need for an inward moral power to enable him to conquer
his sinfulness and live a life that would be pleasing to God. In that
period the prophets criticised the sins of God's people and
advocated their return to his ways. In the next chapter we will
seek to examine their views.

The prophets as ethical teachers

The prophets of the Old Testament were first and foremost God's messengers and his spokesmen. The usual Hebrew word translated into English as 'prophet' is *nabhi* and is derived from a verb meaning 'to call'. The prophet is then a caller, an announcer, a spokesperson. A comparison of Exodus 4:16 and 7:1 shows that Aaron, in the role of spokesman for Moses, was his prophet.

It was the privilege of prophets to receive revelation from the Lord who then spoke his words through them (Amos 3:7, Hos. 12:10). When the Lord so spoke the prophets had to prophesy. As Amos put it – 'who can do other than prophesy?' (Amos 3:8).

Their times

The writing prophets of Israel produced their material over a period of at least 300 years, roughly from the mid-eighth to the mid-fifth centuries BC. They can be divided into six groups on the basis of periods in which they were active:

• *Around 760 BC.* **Amos** and **Hosea**, both of whom served the Lord in and addressed the northern kingdom, Israel, which ceased to exist around 720 BC. The date of **Joel** is disputed but may well have been in the same eighth century. (Later prophets mostly operated in the southern kingdom, Judah.)

• *730 to 680 BC.* **Isaiah** and **Micah** prophesied at a time when the Assyrians were threatening Judah.

• *630 to 580 BC.* **Zephaniah** and **Nahum**, who wrote before the Assyrians were defeated by the Babylonians (612–608 BC) and **Habakkuk** and **Jeremiah** who were somewhat later and wrote after 612 against the background of the Babylonians threatening and in Jeremiah's later years actually conquering Judah.

• *597 to 570 BC.* **Ezekiel**, who wrote as an exile in Babylon. **Obadiah**, whose location is unclear, prophesied against Edom for helping the Babylonians capture Jerusalem (586 BC) and take Jews into exile.

• *530 to 500 BC.* **Haggai** and **Zechariah**, both of whom ministered after the first groups of exiles had returned to Judea. They were most anxious that the temple, which had been destroyed by the Babylonians in 587/6 BC should be rebuilt.

• *460 to 430 BC.* **Malachi** was probably contemporary with Ezra and Nehemiah. He faced social and religious problems among the returned exiles. **Joel**, whom some date as early as 800 BC, is often regarded as belonging to this period.

Their ethical challenges

The ethical demands of the prophets, like those of Moses, are theologically based. They arise in the context of belief in God and knowledge of his character – because God is righteous and 'shows himself holy by his righteousness' (Isa. 5:16) his people must also be righteous. Thus Jeremiah called on his people *to know* the Lord as the one, 'who exercises kindness, justice and righteousness on earth' and who says, 'in these I delight' (Jer. 9:24). Righteousness and right behaviour clearly expressed the fact that a person knew and served God.

Through a vision of the Lord enthroned in heaven, Isaiah became personally convinced that the holiness of God made demands on his own life. He therefore confessed his sinfulness 'Woe to me ... I am ruined!'(Isa. 6:1-8). The revelation of the Lord's holiness convinced him of his own lack of holiness and gave a theological basis to his subsequent ministry in which there is a constant recognition that the Lord is holy – he is 'the Redeemer and *Holy One of Israel*' (Isa. 49:7; cf. 10:17; 29:23).

Micah was deeply concerned about the low moral and spiritual state of his people. He asked what he should bring with him into the Lord's presence – would he bring animal sacrifices? – would he even offer his firstborn to make atonement for his transgressions? The answer to such questions was an emphatic 'No!' What God required was not sacrifice but rather a life of real godliness.

> He has showed you, O man, what is good.
>> And what does the LORD require of you?
> To act justly and to love mercy
>> and to walk humbly with your God (Mic. 6:8).

1. In relation to covenant loyalty

The great burden of these prophets related to the fact that Israel and Judah were persistently disloyal to the covenant between God and themselves. To the terms of this covenant their forefathers had given wholehearted acceptance – 'We will do everything the Lord has said; we will obey' (Exod. 24:1-8). The prophets' primary appeal was, therefore, for a return to the Lord and to loyal observance of the stipulations imposed by him as terms of that covenant.

The Hebrew word *chesedh* which in some English versions is translated by 'mercy' (e.g., Mic. 6:8, Hos. 6:6) is more accurately rendered as 'covenant loyalty', 'covenant faithfulness' or 'steadfast love'. Jeremiah, for example, was commissioned to remind Judah of its covenant relationship with the Lord and to point out that the nation's current problems were due to its failure to be faithful to the terms of that covenant.

> Listen to the terms of this covenant and follow them. From the time I brought your forefathers up from Egypt until today, I warned them again and again, saying, "Obey me." But they did not listen or pay attention; instead they followed the stubbornness of their evil hearts. So I brought on them all the curses of the covenant I had commanded them to follow but that they did not keep (Jer. 11:6-8; cf. Exod. 20-24 and Deut. 1-33 where the stipulations of the covenant are recorded).

What God wanted above all else was faithful adherence to the covenant – he desired mercy (*chesedh*, meaning 'covenant loyalty') and not sacrifice (Hos. 6:6). Faithfulness had been singularly absent as both Israelite and Jew had from time to time mixed the worship of the Lord with that of Baal or of the Babylonian Astarte. God's verdict on the situation was, 'There is no faithfulness, no love, no acknowledgment of God in the land' (Hos. 4:1b).

There is a poignant illustration of Israel's lack of faithfulness in the personal life of the prophet, Hosea, whose unfaithful wife, Gomer, is a picture of the nation in its apostasy or spiritual adultery. Hosea's search for and reclaiming of Gomer from her adulterous relationship (Hos. 3:1-3) is similarly a picture of the Lord's ongoing love for his spiritually adulterous people and of his constant pleading that they would return to him – 'Return, O Israel, to the LORD your God' (Hos. 14:1).

Lack of faithfulness to the Lord inevitably involved serious departure from the manward ethical demands of the covenant that come into focus in the fourth and subsequent commandments. The prophets therefore denounced the serious personal sins and social evils which were characteristic of the age. They constantly called for the ending of practices that denied justice to the poor and the underprivileged. They also demanded the pursuit of righteousness and justice – 'Let justice roll on like a river and righteousness like a never-failing stream!' (Amos 5:24).

2. In relation to personal righteousness

Some scholars have argued that in early Israel family and community solidarity were so strong that there was little sense of individual responsibility and that it was the prophets who brought such responsibility to the fore. The main passages used to support this view are Jeremiah 31:29-30 and Ezekiel 18:1-4. In both it was predicted that an old proverb would cease to be used because of a new covenant the Lord would introduce. No more would it be said, 'the fathers have eaten sour grapes, and the children's teeth are set on edge.' Rather each individual would carry responsibility for his own sins – 'everyone will die for his own sin; whoever eats sour grapes – his own teeth will be set on edge' (Jer. 31:30).

The truth is, of course, that from earliest times individuals were indeed held responsible for their sins. The ten commandments and most of the other Mosaic laws were directed to individuals and the civil penalties prescribed for breaking them were to be applied to offending individuals. Nathan's 'You are the man' brought an intense element of personal responsibility home to David (2 Sam. 12:7). Alongside this there was, of course, a strong family and racial solidarity which meant that the sins of an individual often brought punishment to subsequent generations and even to wider groups. The sins of Achan (Joshua 7) and of David (e.g., when he selfishly counted his people, 2 Samuel 24) provide examples of how this solidarity worked.

Jeremiah and Ezekiel and the other later prophets maintained this two pronged emphasis on personal and corporate or community responsibility. Judah's sin (i.e., its national sin) was engraved with an iron tool (Jer. 17:1). Jerusalem, as a city, would bear the consequences of its detestable practices and the Lord would deal with it as it deserved (Ezek. 16:58f). In the light of these facts we may surely credit the prophets with strengthening individual accountability but not with being its inventors!

The prophets did, of course, criticise and in no uncertain terms call to account individuals, and especially leaders, who acted sinfully. In the earlier period Nathan went straight to the point when he told David that he was 'the man' (2 Sam. 12:7). Amos castigated women who oppressed the poor, who crushed the needy and who lorded it over their husbands (Amos 4:1). Micah was equally forthright when he proclaimed woes on those who plotted evil on their beds and who, by virtue of having power to carry it out, performed it at morning's light (Mic. 2:1f). Isaiah called the rulers of his day companions of thieves and lovers of bribes (Isa. 1:23). He said that they had the plunder of the poor in their houses and had deprived the poor of their rights (Isa 3:14; 10:2).

In a more positive vein we have the later proclamation of Micah – 'he has showed you, O man [i.e., as an individual] what is good.... To act justly and to love mercy [*chesedh* – covenant faithfulness] and to walk humbly with your God' (Mic. 6:8).

Clearly personal righteousness within covenant loyalty to the Lord was the required standard for behaviour and was a most important concern of the prophets.

The later prophets, acutely aware of the failure of the Israelites to live up to their covenant obligations, were the spokesmen through whom the Lord introduced promises of *a new covenant*. Under this, individuals would enjoy a deeply personal relationship with the Lord by virtue of the presence and the workings of his Spirit within them. They would know him and the law would become inward, written on their hearts, and the divine Spirit would move them to follow the Lord's decrees and to keep his laws. He would give them a heart to know him as the Lord – they would be his people and he would be their God (Jer. 24:7; 31:31-34; Ezek. 36:25-29; 37:1-14, cf. Joel 2:28-29).

3. In relation to social justice

While personal and social ethics are not identical they are closely inter-related. Social unrighteousness simply expresses the unrighteous thoughts and emotions of the individuals who make up the society. Often, however, the majority tends to follow the lead of those who influence it by the power of words or example.

Isaiah's response to the vision of the Lord exalted in heaven placed individual and corporate guilt for sin side-by-side. He confessed himself to be a man of unclean lips and to live among a people who were similarly defiled (Isa. 6:5).

The middle years of the eighth century (c770–740) were marked by prosperity in both Israel and Judah. This was accompanied by the acceptance of the standards of a pagan world and by a loss of those social values revealed and, to some degree, learned in the days of Moses. It allowed opportunists to make themselves rich unjustly and even violently at the expense of the poor. Amos in Israel and, later, Isaiah, Micah and Jeremiah in Judah condemned the evils of their times and often sound like modern socialists criticising the financial speculators and the 'fat cats' of a free-for-all capitalist society. Thus we find,

• **Amos** insisting that injustice was an offence against a righteous God (2:6-7). He says:

> They sell the righteous for silver,
> > and the needy for a pair of sandals.
> They trample on the heads of the poor
> > as upon the dust of the ground
> > and deny justice to the oppressed.

Amos went on to accuse his hearers of turning justice into bitterness and of casting righteousness to the ground (5:7). He said that they reduced the size of the measures they used for grain and had underweight scales, thus inflating the price of grain. They were even selling the sweepings with the wheat (8:5-6). At the same time he insisted that justice was a supreme virtue – 'let justice roll on like a river, righteousness like a never-failing stream' (5:24).

• **Hosea,** though contemporary with Amos, was a very different prophet and was mainly concerned with Israel's spiritual apostasy, which he presented as an affront to God's love. For him virtue lay in faithfulness (Hebrew, *chesedh*), truth and a proper knowledge of God (4:1, 6:6). Though he didn't ignore social injustice (e.g., 12:7-8), he did not emphasise it to the extent that the other prophets did.

• **Isaiah,** like Amos, presented injustice as an offence to a righteous God. He insisted that the Lord would enter into judgment against the leaders of his people, because plunder taken from the poor was in their houses and their victims were being crushed into the ground (3:14-15, cf. 1:23, etc.).

• **Micah** had an emphasis very similar to that of his contemporary, Isaiah. One very strong passage reads:

> Woe to those who plan iniquity,
> > to those who plot evil on their beds!
> At morning's light they carry it out
> > because it is in their power to do it.
> They covet fields and seize them,
> > and houses, and take them.
> They defraud a man of his home,
> > a fellow-man of his inheritance (2:1-2, cf. 2:8-9; 6:11-12).

Amos, Isaiah and Micah consistently condemned luxuries, like excessive drinking, which were characteristic of unjust and oppressive people. They also condemned the bribery by which the penalties of civil law could be and were evaded (Amos 2:6-8; 5:12; 6:4-7; Hos. 4:11; Isa. 1:23; 5:22-23; Mic. 3:9-11).

• **Jeremiah** accused the Jews of his day of virtually every social sin that could be imagined. Indeed their social evils were a major factor in the penalty of seventy years exile in Babylon, which was soon to be meted out to them. He said, 'Among my people are wicked men who lie in wait like men who snare birds and like those who set traps to catch men.... Their evil deeds have no limit' (5:26-28 cf. 9:1-9; 22:13-17).

• **Ezekiel**, writing in exile in Babylon, accused the Jews of having broken all ten commandments and, indeed, of many other social offences (22:6-12).

• **Habakkuk** bemoaned the injustice he had observed among his own people and what he thought was God's failure to stop the rot:

> Therefore the law is paralysed,
>   and justice never prevails.
> The wicked hem in the righteous,
>   so that justice is perverted (1:4, cf. 2:6-17).

• **Zephaniah** presented the 'day of the Lord' as bringing retribution on the unjust – Jerusalem's rulers were roaring lions and evening wolves (1:9; 3:3-4).

Putting the evidence together it is impossible to avoid the conclusion that social justice was at a discount in the age of the writing prophets and that its re-establishment was one of their major concerns. Amos surely summarises their emphasis, 'Let justice roll on like a river, righteousness like a never-failing stream' (Amos 5:24).

4. In relation to life in other nations

While the Old Testament is primarily concerned with God's covenant people, Israel, it did not ignore the morality of a wider humanity. The creation ordinances and the precepts given to Noah pre-date the covenant inaugurated by God's promises to Abraham and were meant to apply to all peoples. Because this was so the prophets were properly able to pass judgment on the behaviour of the nations surrounding or impinging on Israel. They assumed a universal moral standard which the nations they criticised should have observed, and for the breach of which God would punish them.

• **Amos** opened his prophecy with oracles denouncing the sins of Damascus, Gaza, Tyre, Edom, Ammon and Moab (Amos 1:3-2:3).

• **Isaiah** maintained that the Lord was using the Assyrians as the rod of his anger to chastise a godless Judah (Isa. 10:5-6). He also pointed out that the Assyrians had a different agenda, namely the destruction of Judah, and that God would punish them for the proud and arrogant way in which they treated their victims (Isa. 10:12). Clearly they were subject to a known moral standard.

In addition Isaiah devoted ten chapters (13-21 and 23) to prophecies about and against foreign nations – Babylon, Assyria, Moab, Damascus (Syria), Cush, Egypt, Babylon (again), Arabia and Tyre. These prophecies assume that those nations were subject to moral standards of which they were aware and on the basis of which they were about to experience the hand of God in judgment.

• **Nahum** concentrated his entire prophecy on the condemnation of the Assyrians. He vividly pictured their ruthless militarism (2:11-12; 3:1-3) and their unmitigated greed (2:9; 3:16) and asserted repeatedly that the Lord would take vengeance on them.

• **Habakkuk** treated the Babylonians in the same way. God was about to use them to chastise Judah, but would also hold them responsible for their plunderings and for the gains they had obtained unjustly (1:5-11; 2:2-20).

• **Obadiah** had a similar message for the Edomites.

• **Jeremiah,** who witnessed the overthrow of Judah by the Babylonians and the beginning of the Exile, concludes his prophecies with six chapters (46-51), in which the Lord affirmed that he would punish the various nations around Israel. Egyptians, Philistines, Moabites, Ammonites, Edomites, Elamites and Babylon all come under the Lord's condemnation as each is declared to be responsible for its social and national sins.

• **Zephaniah** focused on the coming 'great day of the Lord', which would bring wrath to Judah and to a group of five other nations (2:4-15).

Unitedly, then, the prophets proclaimed that the Lord, the God of Israel, was sovereign over all the nations of the world. They saw those nations as accountable to him and to a universally binding standard of right and wrong. In a sense they anticipated the words of Paul:

> For since the creation of the world God's invisible qualities – his eternal power and divine nature – have been clearly seen,... so that men are without any excuse (Rom. 1:20).

Conclusion

The prophets, with their deep insight into the nature of God as infinitely holy and infinitely loving, were channels through whom God revealed himself and his will to men. In the mind and the teaching of each of them, personal and social righteousness was the evidence that an individual or a community knew and served God, the Lord. Holiness among men was a lifestyle that conformed to God's own holiness.

8

The ethics of the Hebrew sages

The ancient world had a great number of sages, who were often called 'the wise'. In written form their sayings and teachings are known as 'wisdom literature'.

The wise were counsellors to kings and other leaders and served as professional or semi-professional tutors to the young. In this role the sage was 'father' and the person he counselled or taught was 'son'. Thus Joseph could tell his brothers that God had made him 'a father to Pharaoh', meaning simply that he had been a counsellor to Pharaoh (Gen. 45:8). The wise tutor we meet in Proverbs and who addressed his pupil as his son, ('my son' – Prov. 1:2; 2:1; 3:1, etc.) was expressing his relationship to that pupil in father-son terms. Among 'the wise' of ancient Israel fatherhood did not necessarily, therefore, denote biological paternity but roles like teaching, advising and counselling.

The apostle Paul thought in a similar way of his work as an evangelist – he had become father to his converts through the gospel (1 Cor. 4:15).

'The wise' were sometimes listed as a distinct class of persons who worked alongside priests and prophets. Thus Jeremiah set the counsel of the wise in the same context as the teaching of the law by the priests and the proclamation of the word by the prophets (Jer. 18:18). Ezekiel similarly associated the ministries of priests and prophets with what he called 'the counsel of the elders' (Ezek. 7:26). The parallel between the two passages suggests that there was a link between 'the wise' and those recognised as elders. The sages may, in fact, have been senior citizens whose long life had given them special 'understanding' and qualified them as 'the wise' (Job 12:12). But in Israel, in contrast to the rest of the Near East, wisdom was not regarded as originating with the sages themselves but with God. He alone was its source. In the Psalms and the Proverbs the fear of the Lord was proclaimed as 'the beginning of wisdom' (Ps. 111:10; Prov. 9:10 etc.). Job said that wisdom and power; counsel and understanding belong to God (Job 12:13).

It is worth noticing that women as well as men were numbered among the wise. The wise woman of Tekoa (2 Sam. 14:2) and another wise woman mentioned in 2 Samuel 20:16 are examples. The noble wife of Proverbs 31:10-31 is another – she speaks wisdom and dispenses faithful instruction; in a word she is a sage.

Their teaching methods

What the sages taught was largely a matter of practical insight into human life and the way it should be lived. They then passed on their wisdom in the form of pithy proverbs. The process by which they operated involved three stages that are explained in Proverbs 24:30-33:

• *Observation*
The sages were careful observers of what went on around them. In this passage one of their number describes what he saw as he looked into a lazy man's garden:

> I went past the field of the sluggard,
>   past the vineyard of the man who lacks judgment;
> thorns had come up everywhere,
>   the ground was covered with weeds,
>   and the stone wall was in ruins (vv. 30-31).

Observation of what went on in life situations ensured that the sages used ideas and terminology that were meaningful and relevant to those they taught. They knew how to be, as we would say, on a wavelength with their hearers.

• *Reflection*
The second step was to think about, to meditate on, what had been observed and to draw out from it a lesson that needed to be taught and learned. Our sage says:

> I applied my heart to what I observed
>> and learned a lesson from what I saw (v. 32).

The product of such meditative reflection was always a firm conviction about a particular aspect of life. These convictions were formulated as proverbs and were the basic element of the sages' teaching or counsel.

• *Instruction*

The sage who wrote Proverbs 24:30-34 put his conclusion as follows:

> A little sleep, a little slumber,
>> a little folding of the hands to rest –
> and poverty will come on you like a bandit
>> and scarcity like an armed man. (vv. 33-34)

As happened in this case the sages formulated their conclusions into pithy sayings (proverbs) which ordinary people, most of whom were illiterate, could remember.

The sages used a variety of literary forms to convey their message. The main one was the proverb (Hebrew, *mashal*). Examples of it fill the book of Proverbs and are found throughout the Old Testament (e.g., 1 Kings 20:11). A special type of proverb, the proverb of blessing, is known as a 'beatitude' (e.g., Ps. 1:1). There is a frequent use of similes (e.g., Proverbs 25:28 where the idea being taught is presented as being *like* something known by those who were being taught). Sometimes the wise taught by means of riddles (e.g., Judg. 14:13) and on several occasions even through invented stories or fables (e.g., Judg. 9:8-15).

Another wisdom technique was to build up a battery of two or more rhetorical questions in order to get some important point across. Two good example are found in Jeremiah:

Questions:	Does a maiden forget her jewellery? a bride her wedding dress? (2:32)
Lesson:	Yet my people have forgotten me, days without number. (2:32)

Questions: Can the Ethiopian change his skin? or the leopard
                  its spots? (13:23a)
Lesson: Neither can you do good who are accustomed to
                  doing evil. (13:23b)

To both pairs of questions everyone listening would answer 'No
– Of course not!' Then came the piercing comments, the point of
which only the most obtuse individual could miss (2:32b and
13:23b).

Another characteristic of wisdom teaching is the contrasting
in one sentence of good and evil, virtues and vices. Thus moral
opposites frequently appear side by side in one verse in a form
which both highlights and warns against wrong attitudes and
actions by contrasting them with right ones. Thus we have,

Hatred stirs up dissension, but love covers all wrongs (Prov. 10:12).

A truthful witness does not deceive, but a false witness pours out
lies (Prov. 14:5).

Their philosophy

Like their contemporaries in other cultures, the Israelite sages
tended to believe that wise living ensured long life and prosperity
(Prov. 16:31) and that foolish and evil ways produced adversity
and disaster. However, they set their teaching firmly in the context
of belief in God. For them, the fear of the Lord was the beginning
of knowledge and wisdom (Prov. 1:7; Ps. 111:10). The Lord gave
wisdom, knowledge and understanding to those who learned from
him (Prov. 2:6).

While the idea that wise living brought prosperity and that folly
produced adversity was widespread, human experience was often
different – the righteous suffered adversity and the unrighteous
enjoyed prosperity! As a result some of the inspired sages had to
grapple with difficult questions. Two psalms (37 and 73), for
example, deal with the prosperity of the wicked, who, on the basis
of wisdom philosophy, should be suffering adversity or even
destruction. The answer of the two psalms is that the experiences

of this life do not represent the full picture and that either later on in life or in the hereafter retribution will overtake the wicked (37:9,13,20,35-38 and 73:27). Prosperity of itself cannot, therefore, be taken as proof that those who enjoy it are morally righteous.

The other side of the problem comes into sharp focus in the book of Job, where Job, clearly a man of wisdom and righteousness, found himself suffering great adversities (chs. 1 and 2). As a result he asked and kept on asking the obvious question, 'Why?' (3:11,12,20,23) or, as we might put it, 'Why me?' In effect he was raising the question, 'Why does a man who does right suffer instead of prospering as wisdom philosophy would dictate?'

Job's three friends held the basic wisdom view and acting more as prosecutors than as friends gradually built up a case against Job. They believed that his sufferings were proof that he had offended God by committing serious sins. Job replied to them one by one and in a series of speech-cycles was more and more provoked by their accusations, which were developed in an ascending scale.

A fourth friend, Elihu, made an attempt to resolve the problem. He was milder than the others but he too failed to solve Job's problem and it was only in direct confrontation with the Lord that Job got an answer (40:1–42:6). That answer was religious rather than intellectual or academic and brought Job to acknowledge God's sovereignty and the fact that under provocation by his sufferings and by his friends he had spoken beyond his understanding and had, in fact, spoken harshly of God. He now despised himself and, bowing before the Sovereign Lord, repented and was restored to God's favour (42:7-17). The fact that Job did not receive an explanation of his sufferings did not matter at all. The important thing was that he learned to trust in the Lord and in his sovereign control of everything that had happened to him.

While it is true that a person often 'reaps what he sows' it is not for others to draw a direct line from one's past behaviour to one's present prosperity or adversity. We just can't explain these things – but we can say that prosperity never proves that a person is righteous and adversity does not prove that he is wicked. Adversity must never be used as the basis of an accusation that someone is being punished for his or her sins.

Jesus endorsed this emphasis from the book of Job when in Luke 13:1-5 he insisted that those who met a gory fate at the hands of Pilate and those who died because a wall had fallen on them did not suffer because of specific sins they had committed. For him it was wrong to think that this had been the case. Indeed he maintained that his listeners were as much in need of repentance as the unfortunate victims of adversity of whom he spoke.

Their moral teaching

The wisdom literature of the Old Testament is part of divine revelation and so has a godward dimension not found in secular wisdom. It developed and applied the two great absolute commands of the Pentateuch – *Love the Lord your God with all your heart and with all your soul and with all your strength* (Deut 6:5) and *You shall love your neighbour as yourself* (Lev. 19:18). These two absolutes are, of course, expanded in the Ten Commandments all of which are endorsed and emphasised in the teachings of the Hebrew sages.

1. Love for the Lord
Wisdom's primary demand was for a right relationship to the Lord – 'the fear of the LORD is the beginning of wisdom' (Prov. 1:7; 2:1-15; 9:10; 24:21). The first three commandments – no other gods, no images representing deity and no misuse of the divine name – were clearly prioritised and reaffirmed by this demand.

2. Love for neighbours
Wisdom also required that those who fear the Lord love their neighbours – oppressing the poor was contempt for the Lord but kindness to the needy honoured him (Prov. 14:31). In developing this emphasis the sages clearly advocated the keeping of God's law. Indeed every verse of a famous wisdom psalm (Ps. 119:1-176), using words like statutes, precepts, decrees or commands, refers to God's law and makes its observance obligatory. For example,

Blessed are they whose ways are blameless,
  who walk according to *the law of the* LORD.

Give me understanding,
  and I will keep *your law* and obey *it* with all my heart (vv. 1, 34).

While an emphasis on law always runs the danger of becoming legalistic (i.e., making acceptance by God dependent on works that are in harmony with law), the wisdom literature itself is not legalistic. It asserts that man's first obligation is to fear the Lord (Ps. 111:10; Prov. 1:7 etc.). A right relationship to the Lord, i.e., one of reverential trust (fear) fixed the context in which divine law and common-sense wisdom principles were to be observed.

Taking the remaining seven commandments one by one we see something of how the sages wove their demands into their teachings.

While the issue of Sabbath observance is not raised, the positive side of *the fourth commandment* appears as a stress on hard work and positive industry. Those who are wise labour diligently in stark contrast to sluggards (lazy persons) who fail to work as they should.

Lazy hands make a man poor,
  but diligent hands bring wealth (Prov. 10:4; cf. 6:6-11; 12:24;
  24:33-34; 26:13-16; 31:12-27).

The fifth commandment is re-affirmed by a stress on the duty of offspring to contribute to the family income by diligent labour:

He who gathers crops in summer is a wise son,
  but he who sleeps during harvest is a disgraceful son
                    (Prov. 10:5, cf. 15:20; 19:26).

The sixth – 'you shall not murder' – is covered by a constant insistence that violence is evil and that people who shed innocent blood are hated by God and spurned by men:

A man tormented by the guilt of murder
  will be a fugitive till death;
  let no-one support him (Prov. 28:17, cf. 6:16-17; 16:27-32).

At the same time the virtues of love, of ordinary human kindness and of peace-making are extolled:

> When a man's ways are pleasing to the Lord,
> > he makes even his enemies live at peace with him (Prov. 16:7,
> > cf. 24:17-18).

The requirement of *the seventh commandment* is presented in terms of a high view of marriage and a zealous and frequent denunciation of adulterous relationships. A good wife is of supreme value (Prov. 18:22; 31:10-31). Faithfulness is required from both husbands and wives. A prostitute is an awful snare and men are frequently warned to avoid the adulteress who is spoken of in strongly derogatory terms:

> Keep to a path far from her,
> > do not go near the door of her house.
> A man who commits adultery lacks judgment;
> > whoever does so destroys himself (Prov. 5:8; 6:32-33, cf. 2:16-
> > 19; 5:1-23; 6:23-35; 23:27-28).

The eighth commandment appears in an emphasis on the seriousness of stealing. Even though there was some leniency for those who stole in order to avoid starvation, such were regarded as responsible for their actions and when caught were expected to pay sevenfold for the offence (Prov. 6:30-31). Even in poverty stealing was regarded as profaning God's name:

> Give me only my daily bread....
> > Otherwise, I may become poor and steal,
> > and so dishonour the name of my God (Prov. 30:8-9).

The ninth commandment is affirmed in calls to avoid false witness and to maintain honest witness. The great concern behind this was that justice should be done.

Associated with honesty of speech is an emphasis on the proper use of the tongue. The sages had no time for the scoffer or slanderer whom they dismissed as troublemakers, abominations and fools:

Drive out the mocker, and out goes strife;
>quarrels and insults are ended (Prov. 22:10, cf. 10:18; 14:6; 21:24; 24:9; 29:8).

In the case of *the tenth commandment* the sages often bring the inner attitudes of the human heart under critical scrutiny. The desires of the sluggard, the oppressor and the adulterer all come under judgment (6:25; 21:25,26). In commending hatred of ill-gotten gain its opposite, greed or covetousness is condemned (Prov. 28:16).

For the sages as for the prophets morality was a matter not just of external conformity to laws and rules but of the inner thoughts of the heart.

3. Job's self-righteous standard

The final response of Job to his three friends, Eliphaz, Bildad and Zophar, (Job 31) shows not just his own standards but those of the wisdom school to which he and/or the writer belonged. Some scholars regard the chapter as the pinnacle of Old Testament morality. Certainly the standard Job displayed is remarkable because it not only reflects an appreciation of the Ten Commandments but in some ways is an anticipation of the ethics of Jesus and the New Testament. However in terms of the inner attitudes Job displayed it needs considerable qualification.

Job's appeal to the Almighty that he might be given a written indictment which he could wear like an epaulet on his shoulder or a crown on his head smacks of incredible cheek and self-righteousness before God (vv. 35-37). He would respond to such a document by parading his innocence – 'like a prince I would approach him!' At this point in the story Job is clearly out of touch with God and is a long way from the penitence he displayed later (chs. 41,42).

Nonetheless his understanding of right and wrong and his claims to right behaviour indicate a quite remarkable ethical standard that deserves careful study. He claimed to:

• *avoid sexual lust (vv. 1-4)*
>but tauntingly challenged the Lord (vv.2-4).

• *maintain personal integrity (vv. 5-8)*
  and challenged God to treat him justly.

• *abstain from adultery (vv. 9-12)*
  and pronounced an imprecation on himself, his wife and
  his harvests if he were guilty of such misdemeanour.

• *have been just to his servants (vv. 13-15)*
  and acknowledged that all are equal before God.

• *care and provide for the poor and the deprived (vv. 16-23)*
  and admitted that the fear of divine punishment kept him
  from neglecting these duties.

 • *avoid worship of material things, of the sun or of the moon
(vv. 24-28)*
  and regarded such worship as sin

• *avoid gloating over an enemy's misfortunes (vv. 29-30)*
  and never cursing such.

• *provide hospitality to travellers (vv. 31-32).*

• *have been open about his sins (vv. 33-34).*

• *avoid 'land-abuse' (vv. 38-40)*
  and again call down adversity on himself if he were guilty
  of environmental vandalism.

In Psalm 15 David sets out a similar high standard of personal
integrity as the basis of a proper relationship with the Lord. His
words are worth quoting it in full:

LORD, who may dwell in your sanctuary?
    Who may live on your holy hill?

He whose walk is blameless
    and who does what is righteous,

who speaks the truth from his heart
    and has no slander on his tongue,
who does his neighbour no wrong
    and casts no slur on his fellow-man,
who despises a vile man
    but honours those who fear the LORD,
who keeps his oath
    even when it hurts,
who lends his money without usury
    and does not accept a bribe against the innocent.

He who does these things
    will never be shaken.

4. Discipline is emphasised

Again and again the wise teacher calls on his pupils to discipline themselves. In the first instance the heart is to be guarded because it is the spring from which the thoughts and the actions of life are motivated:

Above all else, guard your heart for it is the wellspring of life (Prov. 4:23).

Then there is the requirement that parents train their children in such a way that in later life they would apply what they are taught to their own lives and so become properly self-disciplined:

Train a child in the way he should go,
    and when he is old he will not turn from it (Prov. 22:6).

The complementary emphasis is that children should live by the good instruction of their parents:

For these commands are a lamp,
    this teaching is a light,
and the corrections of discipline
    are the way to life (Prov. 6:23).

What is absolutely clear is that the sages called for a disciplined pattern of life based on love for God and for one's neighbours, a

life marked by disciplined godliness, by obedience to the laws of
God, by personal integrity and by justice:

> Speak up for those who cannot speak for themselves,
>   for the rights of all who are destitute.
> Speak up and judge fairly;
>   defend the rights of the poor and needy (Prov. 31:8).

9

The first century scene

When we open the New Testament we find a world very different from that of the Old Testament. There was no independent Israelite or Jewish state. Judea, Samaria and the surrounding areas were all under the control of the Romans. Members of the Herod family, who were unpopular with the Jews, ruled as client Kings over small areas called tetrarchies. One, Herod Archelaus, had Judea and Samaria from 4BC till 6AD when he was deposed. Another, Antipas, the one Jesus called 'that fox', controlled Galilee and Perea throughout the period of our Lord's earthly life.

After they had removed Archelaus and were unable to find a Herod they could trust to rule Judea and Samaria, the Romans appointed one of their own officers as procurator or administrator. Pontius Pilate, who was in that position during our Lord's ministry, is the most famous. Under the procurators Jewish councils called sanhedrins had some responsibility for local affairs and in particular for matters of religion and education.

Jewish perversions of the law

In the period between the two testaments there was great emphasis on the study of the Law. Scribes, who claimed to follow in the footsteps of Ezra (Ezra 7:6,11), became the authoritative Jewish teachers. Sects, mainly the Sadducees and the Pharisees, came into being and formulated a host of rules, which they thought would help their people live in a way that would please the Lord.

Unfortunately the Pharisees and later on their successors, the Rabbis, gave these rules, known as the traditions of the elders, the same authority as the Mosaic Law. Some teachers even said that it was a greater sin to break their traditions than to break the Law of Moses!

The Pharisees were legalists, who attempted to secure God's

favour by what they judged to be works that conformed to their laws. In their view it was vital, for example, that a person did no work and travelled no long distance on the Sabbath. They therefore produced no less than fifteen hundred laws specifying what should *not* be done on that day! Plucking a few ears of corn or relieving the suffering of the chronically ill was work and when it took place on the Sabbath the law was broken!

The pettifogging (petty or hair-splitting) laws or traditions of the Pharisees were constantly multiplying and became the focus of the clash between Jesus and the Pharisees (Matt. 23 etc.). He was not a legalist such as they had become. He wanted an inward righteousness based on good motives, a righteousness that would be better than theirs. He said 'unless your righteousness surpasses that of the Pharisees and the teachers of the law, you will certainly not enter the kingdom of heaven' (Matt. 5:20).

Jewish reliance on traditional laws lies behind Paul's opposition to a group of men who travelled from Judea to Antioch and who tried to force Gentile converts into becoming Jews through circumcision and acceptance of the yoke of the law (Acts 15; Rom. 3:21-31; Gal. 2:11-6:16). In Paul's thought those, who said that faith in Christ was not sufficient and that righteousness could be gained only through accepting and keeping Jewish (i.e, Pharisaic) law, were saying that Christ had died for nothing (Gal. 2:21). In effect theirs was a non-biblical religion, different from that of Abraham and of the worthies of Old Testament faith, whose justification before God was a matter of faith working itself out in faithfulness and loyalty to covenant obligations.

New Testament ethics

Jesus said, 'I have come not to abolish the law or the prophets but to fulfil them' (Matt. 5:17). His coming brought about the fulfilment both of the law and of the prophets and changed the whole picture. Just as the predictions of the prophets about him were fulfilled in his life, death and resurrection so the law in all its aspects was fulfilled in him. Almost certainly this means that God's intention for the whole body of Old Testament law had been realised in Christ. It also means that, in the new order he was initiating, it was his teaching, *the law of Christ* as Paul calls it, which was to be the standard his disciples would be expected to follow.

1. New Testament ethics build on those of the Old Testament

In all its teachings the New Testament builds on the Old, which it accepts as revelation from God. In the case of ethics the essential standards of morality continue unchanged – murder, adultery, theft, false witness and covetousness are still contrary to God's law and are consistently condemned. Indeed it is possible to trace in the New Testament an endorsement of each of the ten commandments, with all of them except the fourth being actually quoted. The fourth was, however, endorsed when our Lord said, 'the Sabbath was made for man.' He clearly affirmed that man needs what the Sabbath provides, i.e., one day of rest after six days of work.

New Testament ethics, like Old Testament ethics, are theologically based. They arise from a knowledge of the character of God and as an obligation to please him by reproducing his own behaviour – Christians are to be perfect as their Father in heaven is perfect (Matt. 5:48). They are to follow our Lord's example (John 13:15; 1 Pet. 2:21) and adopt the same unselfish attitudes as he displayed (Phil. 2:5; 1 Pet. 4:1).

At the heart of the Christian ethic is the fact that authority lies not in man but in God to whom men are obligated. We are required to be holy not because of some man-made standard of behaviour but because our God is holy – 'Be holy, because I am holy' (1 Pet. 1:16, citing Lev. 11:44-45).

2. New Testament ethics are realistic about man's need

The entire New Testament affirms that man is a sinner with an evil heart and quite unable in or of himself to attain to God's standards (Matt. 7:11; Mark 7:21-23; Rom. 3:9-18,23; 5:12; 7:18-25). But, while naturalistic and pseudo-Christian ethical systems leave men to struggle in their own strength towards an unattainable goal of perfection, the New Testament affirms that God gives his servants supernatural power to transform their desires and strengthen their wills. Incidentally modern Judaism also believes that man is able to live righteously and this belief is a major stumbling block in the path of Jews when they are confronted with the claims of Christ and his gospel.

The Christian knows that God works within him and that he can do everything that is demanded of him through Christ who is the source of his strength. He knows that God works within him to empower him to act in harmony with his (God's) purposes (Phil. 2:13; 4:13; John 14:12-27; Rom.7:24-25; Gal. 5:16).

3. New Testament ethics are spiritual in nature

New Testament ethics are not focused on a mere obedience to law, which, however good it may be, cannot of itself make men righteous (Rom. 3:20; Gal. 3:21). They are rather presented as an expression of personal devotion to the Lord. Jesus himself said that the greatest commandment of all is, 'love the Lord your God with all your heart and with all your soul and with all your mind' (Matt. 22:37-38). Those are requirements that focus on a person's inner spiritual life. They are spiritual rather than legal.

The fact that law by itself could not make people righteous or good was already clear in Old Testament times. Its inability to do so led to God's promise of a new covenant under which he would write his law on and put his Spirit in the hearts of people (Jer. 31:31-33; Ezek. 36:26-27). These passages predicted that men would be changed and become inwardly inclined, i.e., inclined in their own spirits, to obey God's laws.

The New Testament shows that these promises were fulfilled in the teachings of Jesus and in the indwelling of the Holy Spirit in the lives of believers. Christians experience God's Spirit changing their hearts (or spirits) and inclining their wills towards righteousness. Thus Paul could tell his Galatian readers that God had sent the Spirit of his Son into their hearts (Gal. 4:6). In our Lord's own words, God gives his believing subjects a Comforter, a Strengthener, who changes their desires and empowers them for holy living (John 14:26; 15:26). The Christian's good behaviour is now a *spiritual* matter based on the presence of God's Holy Spirit within his heart.

4. New Testament ethics involve absolutes but are not legalistic
The Pharisees regarded the observance of laws as the one and only way to please God. To the law of Moses they added traditions declaring this or that bound (i.e., forbidden) or loosed (i.e., permitted).

When the Pharisees accused Jesus' disciples of failing to live according to the tradition of the elders by eating their food without having ceremonially cleansed their hands, he accused them of hypocrisy and of following their traditions rather than the commands of God (Mark 7:1-8). He then accused them of setting aside the fifth commandment by allowing a person to regard money as 'Corban', i.e. a potential gift to God, and so avoid using it to support aged and impoverished parents. By doing this and many similar things they nullified the word of God (Mark 7:9-13).

Jesus said that in expecting people to obey their traditions the Pharisees put heavy (or impossible) burdens on men's shoulders (Matt. 23:4).). He even charged them with shutting the kingdom of heaven in men's faces (Matt. 23:13).

In contrast Jesus offered an easy yoke and a light burden (Matt. 11:30):

> Take my yoke upon you and learn from me, for I am gentle and humble in heart, and you will find rest for your souls. For my yoke is easy and my burden is light (Matt. 11:29f).

Our Lord went beyond the rejection of Pharasaic legalism and actually set aside some Old Testament Mosaic laws. Thus Mark tells us that he 'declared all foods clean' (Mark 7:19). In doing so he was saying that the food laws of Moses would not apply to his followers. Similarly he rendered the Levitical sacrificial laws redundant – he was sacrificed 'once for all' to take away sins and no further sacrifice of atonement would ever be needed (Heb. 9:26).

i) Abiding absolutes
Jesus preached a kingdom in which the only laws were to be those originating in heaven. He said:

What you shall bind (prohibit) on earth shall be what has been
bound in heaven and what you shall loose (leave as not prohibited)
on earth shall be what has been left unbound in heaven (Matt.
16:19, *my translation*).

English versions almost all translate this verse in a way which
makes it say that ethical decisions made by our Lord's followers
on earth would be ratified by God in heaven – 'whatsoever thou
shalt bind on earth shall be bound in heaven ...' (AV). This rendering
of the text is associated with the traditional position of Roman
Catholic theology that Christ gave his apostles and their successors
(the bishops of the church) the right and the duty to make laws for
Christians in every age.

The validity of that translation is, however, open to serious
doubt. The Latin Vulgate, which was translated from Greek around
384-386 AD, rendered the key phrase as 'what you will bind will
be *what has been bound*' (Latin, *ligatum*, the thing having been
bound). In doing so it asserted that what was previously ordained
in heaven and not what scribes, or priests or bishops ordain on
earth was/is the standard to be maintained by those who follow
Christ.

More recently JB Phillips rendered the key clauses by 'whatever
you forbid on earth will be what is forbidden in heaven....' Dr.
Alfred Marshall, in his Interlinear Greek-English New Testament,
also gets the sense accurately – 'Whatever you bind on the earth
shall be (the things) having been (i.e., having already been) bound
in the heavens.'

What our Lord was saying was that his disciples have a duty to
declare what God has already bound or prohibited, in other words
the God-given absolutes of the moral law.

ii) Abiding freedoms

By using the same grammatical construction for 'loosing' as for
'binding' our Lord was also telling his followers that they must
not follow the Pharisees by adding prohibitions of their own to
the absolutes revealed by God from heaven. What heaven had left
loosed or permitted must be left loosed and, therefore, permitted.
Christians must always, therefore, resist the temptation to follow

the Pharisees by insisting on practices and restrictions that are additional to the absolutes already given from heaven and enshrined in the teachings of Christ.

We can say, then, that the previously revealed moral absolutes – love for God and love for neighbours and the expansion of these in the ten commandments stand unaltered and permanently binding. Together with our Lord's own ethical teachings they form what Paul called 'the law of Christ' (1 Cor. 9:21). We can also say that Christians are to avoid promulgating or enforcing rules and regulations (*dos* and *don'ts*) that impose duties additional to those required by heaven on themselves or on their fellow believers.

In harmony with the teaching of our Lord in Matthew 16:18-19 Paul saw himself as what FF Bruce calls 'a free spirit'. In a Jewish environment he could and did subject himself to the rigours of Jewish traditional laws – 'I became like a Jew to win the Jews.' Then in a different situation among Gentiles, who did not have Jewish laws, he behaved as one who did not have those laws (1 Cor. 9:19-23). At the same time he was adamant that he was not a lawless person – he was not free from God's law but was always under Christ's law (1 Cor. 9:21).

In saying this he was asserting that for him and indeed for Christians generally the law of God to which they were obligated was not that of Moses and certainly not that of Pharisaic tradition. It was rather the law of Christ, that is, the law as taught by Christ, who incorporated into his own law the moral absolutes of the older covenant – essentially love for God and for neighbours and the ten commandments.

iii) Paul's use of the word 'law'
In Paul's writings the word 'law' has more than one meaning. He uses it to refer to,

• *the decalogue* (as the ten commandments are sometimes known). It is this understanding of law that underlies his words in Romans 7:7-13, where he says that he would not have known what sin is without the law. Indeed it was by virtue of the law's tenth commandment – 'You shall not covet' – that he became acutely aware of his own sinfulness.

• *the subsidiary moral, ceremonial and civil laws of the Pentateuch.* Indeed those five books collectively are often referred to as 'the Law'. It seems that this is what Luke had in mind when he says that Paul tried from the law of Moses (and from the prophets) to convince Jews in Rome about Jesus (Acts 28:23). It seems also that Paul used law with the same meaning when he says no one will be declared righteous by virtue of observing the law (Rom. 3:20).

For Paul, the law of Moses was essentially good and spiritual (Rom. 7:7,12,14; 1Tim. 1:8-11). It also has an important ongoing function – 'Through the law we become conscious of sin' (Rom. 3:20). He argues that without it (specifically the tenth commandment) he would not have known himself a sinner (Rom. 7:7-8). In addition it has a tutorial role in making men aware of their sinfulness and in bringing them to Christ (Gal. 3:24). To omit it from Christian preaching and teaching is, therefore, to remove something which God desires to use in order to bring men to salvation through faith in Christ.

• *the traditions of Judaism.* These included the laws of Moses and the rules and regulations added to them by the Scribes and Pharisees. These are evidently in mind when Paul speaks of his becoming like a Jew in order to win Jews – 'To those under the law I became like one under the law … so as to win those under the law' (1 Cor. 9:20).

Careful exegesis of Paul's references to law is, therefore, always necessary. It is especially so in passages like Romans 3 and Galatians 3 in which he discusses the place of law in relation to personal salvation. While he rules out law-keeping as the means of salvation, he does not ignore, abandon or devalue divinely revealed moral law.

5. New Testament ethics provide principles for guidance when there is no specific absolute prescription

The Pharisees tried to provide a prescription for every possible situation that life could produce. The New Testament, however, is often content to leave things 'loosed' or permitted and to provide principles the Christian can and should apply in order to discover what is the right course of action in given situations.

i) The glory of God and the good of others

The absolutes of love for God and for one's neighbour (Matt. 22:37-40) make an over-arching framework and a sound starting point. A number of other principles are derived from them. For example,

> Whatever you do, do it all for the glory of God (1 Cor. 10:31).

> In everything, do to others what you would have them do to you (Matt. 7:12).

> Nobody should seek his own good, but the good of others (1 Cor. 10:24).

> Everything that does not come from faith is sin (Rom. 14:23).

> Accord liberty for individuals to differ from each other in the way they behave on matters that are not subject to absolute prescriptions (Rom. 14:1-15:13).

The first three of these statements are intensely positive. They are principles that we must apply to every aspect of our behaviour. The fourth asserts that whatever ethical decisions an individual may have to make must be controlled either by his faith, that is, by what he believes or by his faithfulness, that is, by his loyalty to the Lord. Either way it means that there must be a real knowledge of God and a real relationship with him.

The fifth raises the very important issue of liberty of conscience. The Christian must realise that other believers, perhaps equally sincere and godly as himself or maybe even more so, may think and act differently from himself. In doing so they may still glorify God. Thus, as Paul indicated, some sincere Christians observed special days and others of equal sincerity did not. Some ate animal flesh and others were vegetarians and did not do so, but both groups behaved as they did as a matter of serving the Lord (Rom. 14:6). Similarly in our day some Christians feel it right for them to join their country's armed forces while others are convinced that the commands not to kill others and to love our enemies prevents them from doing so.

The biblical insistence is that in matters that carry no absolute divine prohibition each individual stands or falls before the Lord and not before other Christians. As each has been accepted by Christ so he must accept the others without being judgmental or divisive (Rom. 14:1-15:13).

Application of these principles places a heavy responsibility on the individual. He must think things through for himself and make ethical decisions on the basis of the biblical guidance they give him.

6. New Testament ethics involve self-discipline but not asceticism

In calling men to discipleship our Lord said that they must deny themselves and take up a cross (Mark 8:34). This meant that they must put the honour and the service of Christ before their own honour and their own needs.

Paul's call to live in accordance with the Spirit rather than the sinful nature (Rom. 8:5) brought the same challenge to deny self and give priority to the things of God. His own exercise of self-discipline exemplifies and highlights the point – 'I beat my body and make it my slave so that after I have preached to others, I will not be disqualified for the prize' (1 Cor. 9:27).

The apostle's exercise of self-discipline emerges clearly in his answer to the question he received from the Corinthian church about the eating of meat that had been dedicated in sacrifice to an idol (1 Cor. 8). He knew and most of his readers knew that idols were non-entities and not real gods. They had no power to alter the meat of animals offered to them in sacrifice. So there was nothing inherent in the meat that would prevent a Christian from buying and then eating it, if it was subsequently made available for purchase in a market (vv. 4-6). But there was another side to the picture. Not everyone and not, indeed, some young believers knew that the idol was a non-entity. They thought it represented a god and that meat sacrificed to it became imbued with its power.

For such to eat that kind of meat was to express fellowship with the pagan god and to receive through the meat the power of that god. Paul feared that an immature Christian who didn't yet know that the idol was a total sham might be emboldened to follow the example of more mature believers and buy or eat the meat. Mature Christians would know that it was just animal flesh and nothing more but the weaker ones could eat it as an act of pagan worship and think that it was quite proper to do so because of the example set by more experienced Christians. Because of that danger Paul would discipline himself and avoid such meat:

> Therefore, if what I eat causes my brother to fall into sin, I will never eat meat again, so that I will not cause him to fall (1 Cor. 8:13).

This is not asceticism, which became common in Christendom at a very early stage in its history and which arose from the Greek idea that all matter, including the human body, is evil. Christian ascetics tried and still try to transcend what they suppose to be evil by withdrawing into isolation in order to avoid everything that gives, or that could be thought of as giving, pleasure. In doing so they hope to increase their holiness by going beyond the requirements of the New Testament, beyond those of Christ's law.

The Biblical call to self-denial is different in that it recognises that God has richly provided 'us with everything for our enjoyment' (1 Tim. 6:17). It simply asks that we deny ourselves things that are evil and also such legitimate things as would fail to glorify God or to benefit our fellows (1 Cor. 8-10).

10

Jesus as an ethical teacher (1)

Jesus included a considerable amount of ethics in his teaching and Paul, it will be remembered, spoke of that teaching as 'the law of Christ' or 'Christ's law.' We can rightly think of our Lord as the supreme ethical teacher of all time.

He fulfilled the Law of Moses

In the Sermon on the Mount our Lord said that he had not come to abolish the Law or the Prophets but to fulfil them (Matt. 5:17).

1. His understanding of the law

In speaking of the 'Law and the Prophets' our Lord meant the whole of the Old Testament. For the Jews the Law was the five books of Moses, often referred to as the Pentateuch, while the Prophets would include the rest of the Old Testament. The primary implication of our Lord's words was that law and prophets alike pointed forward to him and found their fulfilment in him.

The religious leaders of our Lord's day and probably also some of his own disciples would think of the Law (Torah/instruction) as including the additional laws introduced by the Scribes. Jesus almost certainly used the word law of the divinely revealed instruction of Old Testament times and only, therefore, of the law of Moses. In the Sermon on the Mount and subsequently, he distanced himself from the extra traditional laws introduced by the Scribes and the Pharisees. He regarded them not as divine laws but as traditions that worked against admitting people into the kingdom of God. (Matt. 15:3, Mark 7:1-13).

2. His fulfilment of the Law

A crucial issue at this point is the meaning of the word 'fulfil'.
Basically the Greek verb *plëroö* has the force of 'filling to the
full', 'completing' or 'bringing about something that had been
predicted or expected'.

In relation to the prophets and their promises of a Messiah
who would come later it is relatively easy to see that Jesus fulfilled
their predictions. Thus, for example, Matthew could say, 'All this
happened to fulfil what the Lord had said through the prophet:
"The virgin will be with child and will give birth to a son and they
will call him Immanuel" – which means "God with us"' (Matt.
1:22f). Jesus was the promised one, the Christ, to whom the
prophets had looked forward.

But how, we ask, are we to understand our Lord's claim that
he had come *to fulfil the law*?

i) By completing in his own person and work the revelation of divine 'Torah' (i.e., instruction).

Grammatically both 'the Law' and 'the Prophets' are objects
of the verb 'fulfil' which must therefore have the same meaning
in relation to both. Jesus was claiming that he filled out or
completed the meaning of the law as well as of the Prophets.

In fulfilling the law Jesus brought the role of the old order (the
Old or Mosaic Covenant), in which God's people were governed
by the law of Moses, to its completion or climax. Indeed he
replaced Moses with a new order, the New Covenant arrangement,
in which God's law would be internalised in the hearts of his people
as had been predicted by Jeremiah and Ezekiel. Whereas under
the Old Covenant God had spoken through prophets, now in the
New he spoke and spoke finally through his own Son (Heb. 1:1,2).
Jesus himself was able to say:

> The Law and Prophets were proclaimed until John. Since then
> the good news of the kingdom of God is being preached (Luke
> 16:16).

In relation to the law what our Lord meant was that his moral
teachings, the laws of his kingdom, were taking over from those

of Moses and becoming the standard by which his disciples would judge conduct.

ii) By including the essentials of Old Testament law in his own teachings

In fulfilling the law Jesus gathered up the essential implications of Old Testament moral law. He cited and endorsed the two greatest commandments requiring love for God and love for neighbours (Matt. 22:34-40 etc.). He quoted with approval nine of the ten commandments and clearly endorsed the principle of the remaining one, the fourth, when he said that Sabbath was made for man. His teachings included, then, the great moral imperatives of Moses and became the standard by which the Christian is to judge conduct. His disciples would be expected to live by those teachings which Paul calls 'the Law of Christ' (1 Cor. 9:21).

iii) By making clear what God intended the law to achieve by observing it fully himself.

He lived a life of perfect conformity to the character of God and to the demands God had made of his creatures in the Old Testament law. At his baptism he expressed a determination to fulfil every demand of righteousness (Matt. 3:15). Later he could even assert his obedience to the law by challenging his critics to prove him guilty of sin (John 8:46).

iv) By highlighting the deep inner meaning of divine law

In his teaching he focused on a righteousness of the heart that would go beyond the outward conformities of the Pharisees and their fellow travellers. In the Sermon on the Mount he made this absolutely clear when he said, 'unless your righteousness surpasses that of the Pharisees and the teachers of the law, you will certainly not enter the kingdom of heaven' (Matt. 5:20, cf. v.48). He demanded a true inner righteousness.

For him anger, hatred and a look prompted by inward lusting are sins of the inner person, of the heart (Matt. 5:22, 28, 43,44). Such sins are the real polluters of a person's life – 'from within, out of men's hearts, come evil thoughts … these evils come from inside and make a man "unclean"' (Mark 7:20-23). Again what matters is a person's inner thoughts and intentions, the state of his heart.

3. His modification of the law

When Jesus asserted that the law would not be done away with till everything of God's purpose for it would be accomplished (Matt. 5:18), his focus was not on the totality of specific laws of Moses. Rather, as indicated already, he was presenting himself and his teachings as that which fulfilled and would take the place of the laws of Moses. It is the precepts he himself taught (in effect his law) that would never pass away. While he picked up and included in his teaching the great moral imperatives of love for God and love for neighbours, he certainly did not mean that every Mosaic precept would remain valid or binding.

In harmony with the divine purpose of fulfilling the law he rendered the Old Testament laws about clean and unclean animals redundant. They had served their purpose and were no longer needed. As Mark tells us 'Jesus declared all foods clean' (Mark 7:19). Similarly his death as a sacrifice for sin rendered the sacrifices prescribed in the Books of Moses obsolete – there was or could be no further sacrifice for sins (Heb. 10:26). As a result of his fulfilment of the law these and any other Old Testament regulations, laws that he did not affirm as putting obligations on his disciples, are not to be regarded as binding on Christians.

In effect the new order had begun. Under it Jesus' own teachings, which leave behind some elements of the Old Covenant law and which bring to the fore the deeper implications of moral living (Matt. 5), are the principles and precepts that are to guide his followers and that are never to pass away. They form what Paul later called 'Christ's law' or 'the law of Christ' (1 Cor. 9:21, Gal. 6:2).

The Christian and the law

The place of law in the Christian life and in its ethic has perplexed many Bible scholars down the ages. They found it difficult to reconcile our Lord's insistence that not even the smallest letter of the law would disappear till all had been accomplished with Paul's statement that he (Christ) is the end of the law (Rom. 10:4).

Some have failed to understand how fulfilment of the law of Moses meant the introduction of the new gospel era (Luke 16:16). Jesus effected a transition from the era of Mosaic law to the spiritual and moral order of the kingdom of heaven. That new order, as we have seen, gathered up in itself and re-emphasised not all the laws of Moses but its essential spiritual and moral imperatives. There was thus no abandonment, no setting aside, of the moral law. But as the succeeding verses in Matthew 5 indicate, there was a clear rejection of the extras that the Pharisees and their fellow-travellers had added to the laws of Moses.

In the case of Romans 10:4 the Greek word translated 'end' is *telos* meaning the terminus or the goal to which something moves. Paul was contrasting the current Jewish idea that salvation was achieved by law observance with the new Christian emphasis on 'righteousness that is by faith'. As far as he was concerned the role of the law as understood by Jews was at an end – it had reached its terminus and the Law of Moses itself had its fulfilment in Jesus. Thus understood, Paul is essentially affirming what Christ had said and there is no conflict between Matthew 5:17-18 and Romans 10:4.

In the nineteenth and early twentieth centuries many Bible teachers adopted the ideas of J.N. Darby. They tried to solve what they thought was a problem by saying that the Sermon on the Mount and any other legal references in the teachings of Jesus related not to the age of the church but to a different phase in the divine administration in the world. They said that Jesus offered God's Plan A (his new system of law or new *dispensation*) to the Jews of his day in the Sermon on the Mount. They rejected it and as a result God's Plan B (the church age) was introduced and implemented. It was argued that Plan A would only become operational in a yet future (Millennial) age.

In support of these ideas it was argued that Christians are not under any form of law and texts like 'sin shall not be your master because you are not under law but under grace' (Rom. 6:14) were cited. Unfortunately this view easily degenerated into antinomianism (opposition to all law observance). It is highly unsatisfactory because it can be used to justify what in Biblical terms is quite immoral behaviour. Oswald Sanders tells, for example, of an Australian man who during World War II went to church on Sundays dressed in black and carrying a large black Bible and who was nicknamed the 'biggest Bible-basher in town'. But he also had a reputation as being the biggest black-marketeer in the town! When challenged about his behaviour he 'replied with complete aplomb: "But I am not under law, I am under grace"' (*The World's Greatest Sermon*, p.47).

It needs to be said that nowadays many Dispensational scholars agree with those of other schools in acknowledging that our Lord was inaugurating a spiritual and moral kingdom made up of all who believe in and follow him as his disciples. They realise that the Sermon on the Mount, in fact, sets out the laws of that kingdom (Christ's law again) and shows disciples and potential disciples the kind of life he expects them to live as its citizens.

The inwardness of morality

1. In relation to righteousness
The new covenant promised through Jeremiah and Ezekiel looked forward to God's law being written on the hearts of people who would truly know him. They would do so through a living relationship effected by an indwelling presence in their lives of his Holy Spirit and would as a result be inclined to do what is right (Jer. 31:33f.; Ezek. 36:26f).

Our Lord's teaching fulfilled this expectation both by drawing out the inward implications of true morality and by rejecting a goodness that was merely an outward mask covering hearts filled with evils and bowed down by an ever-growing package of traditions. He required an inward righteousness of good intentions and pure motivation that surpassed the outward righteousness of the Pharisees (Matt. 5:20). For him morality, good or bad, was an inward reality, a matter of the heart, of desires and of motives, before it was a matter of words or actions.

Jesus regarded the command to love God with the whole being

as the greatest, the most important, of all commandments (Mark 12:28-34). Love for God, an attitude of heart expressing itself in worshipping and serving him, was our Lord's priority. Men were to obey that command with the whole personality, heart, soul, mind and strength.

His second requirement was love for neighbours. This focuses on caring concern and caring action aimed at meeting a neighbour's need or needs. The love in view (Greek, *agapë*) is not sentimental or sexual in nature, but a rational recognition of a neighbour's need and a deliberate effort to care for him whether he is likeable or not, whether he is a friend or an enemy (Matt. 5:43-47). It is essentially an attitude of the heart, which expresses itself in outward action and was tellingly illustrated in our Lord's story of the Good Samaritan (Luke 10:25-37) – the priest and the Levite lacked *agapë* while the Samaritan radiated it!

The teacher of the law, who asked Jesus to indicate the most important commandment, acknowledged that the inward attitude required by these absolutes was of more value than outward observance of the Jewish sacrifices. Clearly that man had better insight into the mind of God than most of his contemporaries. Little wonder Jesus responded by telling him that he was 'not far from the kingdom of God' (Mark 12:32-34). That the lawyer was moving in the right direction was shown by his awareness of the inwardness of morality.

The Sermon on the Mount provides a clear overall picture of our Lord's view that virtue is a matter of inner attitudes. The Beatitudes (Matt. 5:3-10), with which it begins, illustrate this most effectively – blessed, happy or, as the Old Testament background suggests, 'guided aright' are those who conform inwardly to these ideals. (The Hebrew word *ashere* is translated by 'blessed' in Psalm 1:1 etc., but it is derived from a verb meaning 'to walk straight' along the right pathway.) The Beatitudes therefore focus on the blessings of those who are correctly guided through life and who as a result are assured of arriving at their desired destination, the kingdom of heaven. They present an eight-point picture of the kind of attitudes Jesus expected in those who would become citizens of his kingdom.

Blessed or guided aright, then, are

• *'the poor in spirit'* – those whose inner spirits are aware of their total spiritual poverty, who know they need God's mercy and who, like beggars looking to a benefactor, depend entirely on that bounty.

• *'those who mourn'* – those who grieve inwardly over the effects of sin in their own and other lives.

• *'the meek'* – those of humble spirit who accept correction from God and from other human beings.

• *'those who hunger and thirst for righteousness'* – those who yearn to please God and seek him as their top priority.

• *'the merciful'* – those who, having received mercy, are kind and gentle and forgiving towards others.

• *'the pure in heart'* – those whose motivation is single-minded love for God and neighbours. Their desires, their wills and, therefore, their actions are not adulterated by motives of selfish greed or by malice towards others.

• *'the peacemakers'* – those who concern themselves with the total wellbeing of others. In the Jewish mind peace (*shalom*) is wellbeing in every department of life, physical, marital, family, business, social and religious. Peacemakers make peace by the sheer breadth of their care.

• *'those who are persecuted because of righteousness'* – those who face opposition of any kind and in particular persecution and false accusations such as our Lord envisaged in the next verse (v.11).

Moving on, our Lord insisted that the righteousness of the Pharisees and of the other teachers of the law was inadequate. Those who would enter the kingdom of heaven must have a righteousness that excels the outward observances of these groups. It was not enough to be innocent of physical sins like murder, adultery, wrongful divorce or empty oaths (Matt. 5:21-48). Disciples must, in fact, have positive goodness and reproduce the perfections of their Father in heaven (v.48).

From this our Lord went on to focus on three specific areas of life in which the Pharisees showed their lack of inward righteousness. They gave alms publicly, they prayed in public and they fasted in public and they did these things purely in order to be seen by other men and thus applauded for their righteousnesses. Jesus said that they receive their reward in full in this applause but heaven takes no notice of them or of their external piety.

Our Lord's disciples must be totally different:

> Be careful not to do your 'acts of righteousness' before men *to be seen by them*. If you do, you will have no reward from your Father in heaven....when you give to the needy, do not let your left hand know what your right hand is doing, so that your giving may be in secret. Then your Father, who sees what is done in secret, will reward you (Matt. 6:1-4).

Similar instruction follows in relation to both prayer and fasting (Matt. 6:7-18). What our Lord wants is not merely outward observances but a heart of love inwardly inclined to do what is right, not to boost a person's own ego but as an expression of love for God and for one's neighbours.

Later in the Sermon on the Mount our Lord summed up the essentials of good person-to-person relationships in the golden rule of Matthew 7:12 – 'in everything, do to others as you would have them do to you.' Our Lord wants us to express caring kindness and caring action for the benefit of others. This obligation forces us to think about our neighbour's needs and to work for their maximum well-being.

2. In relation to evil

For the Pharisees a sinner was not necessarily a moral offender but simply someone who stood aside from their traditions and ceremonials. By contrast our Lord taught that sin, like virtue, was an issue of the heart, a matter of wrong attitudes and wrong motivation. A man sins not just when he kills another but when he allows his thoughts towards the other to be thoughts of hate, of lust or of deceit (Matt. 5:21-47).

Many of our Lord's parables highlight the sinfulness of neglecting to act positively towards others in times of need. Examples are the rich man who neglected the poor beggar at his gate (Luke 16:19-31) and the priest and Levite, who passed by the injured man on the road to Jericho (Luke 10:25-35). Describing ultimate judgment in terms of the separation of sheep from goats, Jesus said that those who failed to provide food, water and clothing to those in need would be regarded as guilty of not caring for himself (Matt. 25:31-46).

The religion of the Pharisees lacked not just inward reality but basic humanity. Thus they criticised our Lord and his disciples for plucking and eating grain on a Sabbath day when they were hungry (Matt. 12:1-14; Mark 2:23-28). Similarly they objected when he healed the chronically ill on the Sabbath (Mark 3:1-6, John 5:1-18 etc.) and when he sat down to eat with non-Pharisees whom they regarded as sinners (Matt. 9:10-13). They had little or no inner love for others, no real humanity.

In Mark 7:14-23 our Lord spoke of sinful attitudes that arise in the human heart and that are the real defilers of the soul. Some of these negatives involve outward acts of wickedness, but for our present purposes we can pick out those that express the inner thoughts and intentions of the heart.

• *'evil thoughts'* – i.e., schemings of the mind that produce acts of wickedness and revenge.

• *'greed'* – i.e., 'covetings' or desires to acquire possessions and to have advantages over others. The story of the rich fool (Luke 12:13-21) follows and illustrates our Lord's warning to his hearers that they should be on their guard against covetousness or greed (v.15).

• *'malice'* – hateful or malicious thoughts that lead to wicked actions. The Pharisees, who sought to trap Jesus in his words, did so because they had malice in their hearts (Matt. 22:15ff).

• *'deceit'* – thoughts aimed at conquering others by cunning craftiness and sheer dishonesty. Nathaniel was free of it – he was one in whom there was no deceit or guile (John 1:47).

• *'envy'* – thinking of the successes of others with jealousy or of their misfortunes with satisfaction. The Greek idiom our Lord used is that of 'having an evil eye'.

• *'arrogance'* – a showing off of oneself as superior to others – a disdain for those one regards as inferior almost inevitably accompanies this inner vice. Such arrogance is what lies at the root of every form of bigotry and racism.

• *'folly'* – literally being without the wisdom that learns from life and from divine revelation. Such a lack produces moral blindness and an attitude that reverses moral values, regarding good as bad and evil as righteousness. In Romans 1:22-32 Paul vividly describes how it has affected the attitudes and the actions of men and women since time immemorial.

In the light of these portrayals of evil we can say that, for our Lord, sin is an expression of a heart that is self-centred, that puts self before God and before neighbours. Because of this basic defect in human nature, i.e., its selfishness, Jesus called for self-denial on the part of all who would be his disciples.

If anyone would come after me, he must deny himself and take up his cross and follow me (Matt. 16:24).

11

Jesus as an ethical teacher (2)

Our Lord's words and actions clearly indicated the kind of conduct he regarded as good and right. He was not merely sinless but positively virtuous. Indeed his teaching and his life demonstrated the true nature of virtue.

The virtues he taught

1. Humility
In Matthew 11:29 Jesus referred to himself as 'meek and lowly' (AV) or 'gentle and humble' (NIV). The Greek words mean without either personal pride or an ostentatious display of one's own abilities or authority. Such indeed was Jesus.

We remember how in the Upper Room, when the disciples had omitted to arrange for a slave to perform the common courtesy of feet-washing, he rose and himself washed their feet. We can imagine the embarrassment of the disciples when the host at the Passover celebration took on the functions of a slave. At first Peter found it impossible to allow him, his Lord and Master, to wash his feet. Having washed the feet of the twelve disciples Jesus turned the example he had set into a command to his disciples:

> Now that I, your Lord and Teacher, have washed your feet, you also should wash one another's feet. I have set you an example that you should do as I have done to you (John 13:14-15).

In addition Jesus taught that his followers should be humble. He pointed to a young child and said, 'whoever humbles himself like this child is the greatest in the kingdom of heaven' (Matt. 18:4). On another occasion he warned his disciples against taking or using titles like 'Rabbi', 'Father' or 'teacher.' Use of such titles was an indication of the user's pride and was a challenge to the position of God as the one Father and to that of Jesus as the one teacher, 'the Christ'. To drive the point home our Lord said, 'The greatest among you will be your servant. For whoever exalts himself will be humbled and whoever humbles himself will be exalted (Matt. 23:8-12). We today must be careful that we do not allow ourselves to use titles or any other image-boosting tactic as a means of exalting ourselves.

2. Integrity

The sixth beatitude – 'Blessed are the pure in heart' – focuses on single-mindedness and powerfully emphasises the necessity for total integrity in Christian living. It is those who can honestly say, 'one thing I do ... I press on towards the goal ...' who are the pure in heart. As Paul goes on to say, 'All of us who are mature should take such a view of things' (Phil. 3:13-15). It is those who single-mindedly seek first God's righteousness and who do not try to worship God and material things at the same time, who are the 'pure in heart' and who will see God.

Our Lord insisted that his disciples must be persons of honesty in all their relationships. He directed words of Isaiah to the Pharisees as proof that they were hypocrites:

Isaiah was right when he prophesied about you hypocrites; as it is written: 'These people honour me with their lips, but their hearts are far from me. They worship me in vain; their teachings are but rules taught by men' (Mark 7:6-7).

Luke tells us of three men who offered to follow Jesus (Luke 9:57-62). Each was told that to do so demanded total commitment – there might be no bed on which to sleep and no opportunity to care for and ultimately to bury an ageing parent or even to say farewell to one's family. What mattered was total commitment to Christ and the integrity to see that commitment through to the end. The disciple is to be a man of his word:

No-one who puts his hand to the plough and looks back is fit for service in the kingdom of God (Luke 9:62).

An important insight into the hypocrisy of the Pharisees emerges in Luke 16:13-31. Our Lord declared that no servant can with integrity serve two masters. Such a servant is bound to have divided loyalties! Then Jesus added the penetrating adage, 'You cannot serve both God and Money.' He meant that a person cannot at one and the same time worship God and live a life based on monetary or materialistic values. The Pharisees to whom he was speaking then sneered at him because they 'loved money'. They made much of serving God by observing external laws but there was no integrity. Their hearts were not really in their much vaunted service of God because their primary devotion was to money. To drive the message home our Lord told the story of the rich man and Lazarus. In it the rich man, who ended up in Hell, almost certainly portrayed the money-loving Pharisees whose religion lacked integrity.

3. A forgiving spirit

Our Lord didn't vengefully pursue those who wronged him. Rather he left an example to be followed by all his disciples – 'he did not retaliate, ... he made no threats' (1 Pet. 2:21-23). Instead he asked God, his Father, to forgive his tormentors because, as he said, they did not know what they were doing (Luke 23:34).

i) A Christian duty

Jesus strongly emphasised the fact that his disciples have a duty to forgive one another. He instructed them to pray that they might be forgiven their debts as they had also forgiven those in debt to them (Matt. 6:12 etc.). Then he made it plain that a willingness to forgive and an actual forgiving of others were vitally important aspects of discipleship:

> For if you forgive men when they sin against you, your heavenly Father will also forgive you. But if you do not forgive men their sins, your Father will not forgive your sins (Matt. 6:14,15).

In a similar vein Jesus told Peter that an offending brother should be forgiven again and again and again – 'till seventy-seven times' (Matt. 18:22). The parable that follows tells of a king who forgave one of his servants an enormous debt ('over a million pounds' – NIV footnote). The servant had pleaded on bended knees for time to repay his debt, but the master did much more than allow him the time he wanted. He released him completely from the debt!

But then that same man tried to recover a tiny debt owed to him by a fellowservant. Despite that colleague making virtually the same appeal as he had made to the king – 'be patient, give me time and I will pay it back' – he refused to forgive the petty debt ('a few pounds' – NIV footnote). When the king heard what his servant had done, he became angry and punished the offender by cancelling the forgiveness he had earlier granted him.

The implication of the passage is that a disciple of the Lord ought to be a forgiving person and can't expect further forgiveness from God unless he forgives others – 'this is how my heavenly Father will treat each of you unless you forgive your brother from your heart' (Matt. 18:35). In a word he was saying that his disciples couldn't expect God to forgive them if they hadn't in their hearts forgiven others.

On another occasion, when Jesus was teaching his disciples, he used words that effectively summarise his teaching on the duty of Christians to forgive one another and on the extent to which and the circumstances in which they must do so:

> If your brother sins, rebuke [or warn or admonish] him, and if he repents forgive him. If he sins against you seven times in a day, and seven times comes back to you and says, 'I repent,' forgive him (Luke 17:3,4).

ii) An important illustration

The father in the story of the prodigal son also illustrates the virtue of a forgiving spirit (Luke 15:11-32). Forgiveness was in his heart and, when he saw his wayward son in the distance, he ran and embraced him and restored him to his place as a son. He didn't, and indeed couldn't, restore the portion of inheritance which the prodigal had already claimed and squandered. Rather everything remaining in his possession would pass to his elder son (v.31).

But he did freely and gladly forgive the younger one, who had so lamentably disgraced the good name of the family.

iii) A recurring question

It is often asked if we, as Christians, can forgive those who have offended us without first receiving their repentance. In response we can say that the father of the prodigal had forgiveness in his heart before the prodigal returned to him. In the context Jesus clearly meant that father to be a picture of his own Father in heaven and of the fact that he has forgiveness in his heart towards his wayward and sinful creatures. In Christ's death on the cross he purchased forgiveness for them before they knew to repent and believe – 'when we were still powerless, Christ died for the ungodly.... While we were still sinners Christ died for us' (Rom. 5:6-8). Similarly Jesus himself expressed forgiveness towards those who crucified him even though he saw no evidence that they were repentant before him (Luke 23:34).

Forgiveness can, then, be a reality in the heart of an offended person before the one offending him repents, but it is only when repentance occurs that reconciliation and a restored relationship can be enjoyed. The prodigal had to gather himself together, get up and trudge the weary road home to his father and there honestly confess that he had greatly sinned. The sinner, whom God has already redeemed and forgiven in Christ, must turn from his sinful ways, must repent and come in simple childlike trust to his heavenly Father, crying out, 'Lord, be merciful to me a sinner.' Only then can he enter into the enjoyment of forgiveness and reconciliation with God.

Similarly today we can and must forgive those who offend us. We must release ourselves from the feeling that the offender owes us a debt and accept in our hearts that the offence is not going to make us bitter, angry or retaliatory towards the offender. We must leave the matter of judgment to the Lord as Paul enjoined his readers in Corinth – 'judge nothing before the appointed time; wait till the Lord comes' (1 Cor. 4:5). But if we forgive in our hearts then as and when an offender comes to us in repentance, reconciliation and fellowship can be restored instantly. Forgiveness can be one-way but reconciliation is two-way and depends on the offender's repentance.

That said, we need to remember that offences are often, perhaps almost always two-way matters. It may be that a small indiscretion is misunderstood and begins a chain of antagonism that leads to some major crisis, in which one party emerges as the overt offender. But in actual fact both parties have been guilty of giving offence and both need to repent and seek forgiveness. Each needs to forgive the other and only when both do so and do so from the heart does reconciliation become a reality.

4. Family stability

As a child our Lord received tender care in the family of Mary and Joseph. When he was twelve he went with them and was presented in the temple in Jerusalem. Subsequently he detached himself from Joseph and Mary and stayed in Jerusalem listening to and questioning the temple teachers. When Joseph and Mary returned and found him, he readily submitted to them and returned with them to Nazareth. Luke tells us that he was obedient to them (Luke 2:51). Later, as he suffered on the cross, he committed his mother to the care of John, the disciple he loved (John 19:25-27).

Family life was obviously important to him. His respect for it is further shown by his teaching against the break-up of marriage. Though he seems to have permitted divorce to the victim of marital unfaithfulness (Matt. 5:32, 19:9), his main concern was that it should not happen – 'what God has joined together, let man not separate' (Matt. 19:6). His aim was to encourage stable marriages and stable family life.

Our Lord's treatment of and comments about children further emphasise the importance of family life. 'Whoever welcomes a little child like this in my name welcomes me' – 'Let the little children come to me, and do not hinder them, for the kingdom of heaven belongs to such as these' (Matt. 18:5; 19:14).

On one occasion, in debate with Pharisees and teachers of the Jewish law, Jesus scathingly illustrated the way in which they let go of God's commandments in favour of their own traditions (Mark 7:9-13). They allowed a man to say that the money he would have used to support his elderly parents was 'Corban' (Hebrew, *qarban*, an offering brought before the Lord as a free-will gift or sacrifice. See Leviticus 1:2). Under the rabbis the word came to be used not just of an offering but of a vow indicating the intention to make it later. This meant that money or property treated in this way was regarded as devoted to God and not, therefore, available for its normal purposes. By making such a vow a man could perversely avoid his responsibilities to his parents. Our Lord accused the Pharisees of nullifying the word of God by this tradition and in the process affirmed the duty of supporting parents when they become unable to support themselves. In exposing the scandal of Pharisaic tradition Jesus provided another strand in his teaching to encourage stable family life (Mark 7:9-13).

At the same time it must be remembered that our Lord did not regard family life as the absolute priority for his followers. Love for God and devotion to his righteousness and his cause came first. In keeping with this he withstood and publicly distanced himself from his mother and his siblings when they tried to 'take charge of him' because they thought he 'was out of his mind'. He insisted that devoted and obedient disciples had now become his family (Mark 3:21,31-35).

He also pointed out that discipleship can, and sometimes does, cause rifts in the family. He had come to turn a man against his father, a daughter against her mother. The important thing is that he has priority in the affections of his disciples: 'anyone who loves his father or mother,...his son or daughter more than me is not,' he said, 'worthy of me' (Matt. 10:37-39). The three men addressed in Luke 9:57-62 were challenged to put that principle into practice and put Christ before personal comforts and family loyalties.

Clearly, then, while family stability is tremendously important a balance has to be struck between loyalty to it and the requirements of discipleship.

5. Care for the underprivileged

Jesus condemned the Pharisees not for giving alms but for doing so in public. He encouraged his followers to give their alms in secret, not even letting their left hands know what their right hands were doing (Matt. 6:2-4). His condemnation of the uncharitable rich man (Luke 16:19-31) focused on the fact that he ought to have been generous towards the poor man begging at his gate. His picture of the judgment in Matthew 25 presents the righteous as those who had ministered to him by meeting the needs of people around them, and the selfish as those who had not offered hospitality, food, drink, clothing and shelter to needy strangers (Matt. 25:34-46).

In the Sermon on the Mount he said, 'Give to the one who asks you, and do not turn away from the one who wants to borrow from you' (Matt. 5:42). He also proclaimed his golden rule, 'in everything do to others what you would have them do to you' (Matt. 7:12). This means that, when we see others in need, we should treat them with the kindness and generosity we would like to receive if we were in a similar situation.

Jesus ministered to and improved the lot of social outcasts – lepers (Mark 1:40-42) and those who had to resort to begging because of blindness (e.g., Bartimaeus, Mark 10:46-52). He healed the deaf and the paralysed and other unfortunate people who, like the blind, often had no option other than begging. He cast demons out of people, like the man who called himself Legion and who lived in a cemetery and whose strange behaviour made him an outcast from society (Mark 5:1-17).

Our Lord didn't confine his kindness to his own Jewish people but was able to cross over cultural divisions and racial barriers. He healed a Samaritan of leprosy and liberated the daughter of a Syrophoenician woman whose life was blighted because of possession by a demon (Mark 7:24-30).

In ministering to those who were disadvantaged and despised – the poor, the sick, the handicapped and the stranger or alien – Jesus was again setting an example to his followers. He was also making himself a model to be copied by succeeding generations of disciples.

6. Submission to civil authorities

Jesus was not a politician and offered no political manifesto. His kingdom was not of this world. Yet he displayed a clear sense of responsibility to obey the authorities in whose territories he lived and worked. In the context of Jewish demands he made provision to enable the temple-tax to be paid both for himself and for Peter (Matt. 17:24-27). In what seems to be a reference to the demands of Roman soldiers, who compelled people to carry burdens for them, he said, 'if someone forces you to go one mile, go with him two miles' (Matt. 5:41). In relation to what must have been a sensitive issue – paying tax to the Romans – he said, 'Give to Caesar what is Caesar's and to God what is God's' (Mark 12:17).

When he was being arrested and crucified, he accepted the right of the civil authorities, Jewish and Roman, to act in that way and neither resisted them nor allowed his disciples to do so. When Peter took a sword and used it against a servant of the high priest Jesus commanded him to put it away and miraculously restored the amputated ear to the victim of Peter's misguided zeal (Matt. 26:51-54; Luke 22:50, 51; John 18:10, 11). He then insisted that, because he had been given a cup of suffering which he had to drink, no attempt should be made to protect him from what he was about to endure. He thus reacted non-violently to governing authorities even when those authorities were being violent towards him.

This is not to say that Jesus endorsed every action of either the Jewish or the Roman authorities. It is to say that he submitted to civil authorities in all matters that did not involve compromise of his duty before his Father in heaven. When such compromise was demanded he was prepared to take whatever consequences the authorities might impose on him. Ultimately that stance meant death on a cross! He would surely have endorsed the response of Peter and John to the Sanhedrin in Jerusalem – 'we must obey God rather than men' (Acts 5:29).

The vices he censured

Our Lord strongly condemned a wide variety of sinful actions. Such acts are not, however, as prominent in his teaching as in Paul's writings. This may have been because God's law was better known and more widely kept in Palestine than in the Gentile world in which Paul usually worked.

In the Sermon on the Mount (Matt. 5-7), for example, Jesus passed condemnatory judgment on murder (5:21-26), adultery (5:27-30) and, in the context of swearing on oath, false witness (5:33-37). He also warned his disciples against wrongful divorce and consequent wrongful remarriage (5:31-32, cf. Matt. 19:1-9). He told them that rather than repaying evil with acts of revenge his followers should be ready to suffer further indignity (5:38-42). He commanded them not to parade their piety as the Pharisees were doing (6:1-18) and to avoid judging others when their own vision was blurred by virtue of weaknesses and sins in their own lives. He illustrated this by saying that no-one can see a speck in another person's eye when there is a plank or some other blind-fold over his own eyes! (7:1-5).

In describing what it is that defiles a man's character (Mark 7:14-23) our Lord again included sinful actions, that are prohibited by the sixth, seventh, eighth, ninth and tenth commandments. These are sexual immorality (the seventh), theft (the eighth and the tenth), murder (the sixth), adultery (the seventh), greed (the tenth), malice, deceit and slander (the ninth).

The stories of the rich farmer (Luke 12:16-21) and of the rich man in Hades (Luke 16:19-31) both show that it is foolish to make the possession of material things the goal of one's life. 'You cannot', he said, 'serve God and money' because serving two masters leads to love for one and to neglect of the other. He is saying that those who love money or other earthly possessions inevitably have little or no real love for God.

Summing up Jesus' ethics

Jesus was not a legalist, he was unlike the Pharisees who made obedience to Torah (Old Testament law plus their own traditions) the key to life. Neither was he an antinomian (one who abandoned all observance of law). He struck a careful balance between fulfilling divine absolutes and expressing loving care and sympathy to men and women struggling in their fallenness and inability with the temptations and hurts of life.

While he did nothing to impair social authority and was certainly not a violent revolutionary, his teaching exposed and undermined many of the evils of which individuals in positions of authority in his day were guilty. Zacchaeus the tax collector was one who heeded our Lord's teachings and who sought to put right what he had done wrong (Luke 19:8).

We can say that our Lord exemplified and called for the highest ethical standards. In his own life he was determined to fulfil, and indeed did fulfil, all the demands of true righteousness (Matt. 3:15). In his ministry he was concerned to see the kingdom of God established in the hearts of men and women who would then live lives of godliness and true morality. He set an example that disciples in every age are meant to follow.

12

Paul's pattern for Christian living

Paul's letters were addressed to people who lived in the Eastern Mediterranean world and who faced practices not often encountered in Palestine. Because of this the apostle sometimes used different terms from those in the Gospels but essentially his teaching was the same as that of the Lord.

Paul's ethics are essentially a matter of expounding and applying the teachings of the Master, the Lord Jesus Christ. Like Jesus, he gives priority to the inner attitudes that motivate outward actions and especially to love both for God and for neighbours.

Somewhat strangely, however, he doesn't quote or even allude, as Jesus often did, to the command of Deuteronomy 6:5 – 'Love the LORD your God with all your heart.' He rather transferred its focus to Christ, love for whom, he insisted, is an essential mark of true biblical faith. Thus the closing benediction of his letter to the Ephesian Christians prayed: 'Grace to all who love our Lord Jesus Christ with an undying love' (Eph. 6:24). Love for Christ was so important that he was prepared to pronounce an anathema on those who lacked it: 'If anyone does not love the Lord—a curse be on him' (1 Cor. 16:22).

In our Lord's teaching, love for neighbours was the other vital ingredient of a life that pleases God. In relation to this Paul both quoted the command of Leviticus 19:18 (Gal. 5:14) and alluded to it in statements like, 'Let no debt remain outstanding, except the continuing debt to love one another ...' (Rom. 13:8-10) and 'you yourselves have been taught by God to love each other' (1 Thess. 4:9). Paul's great hymn extolling the virtue of love (1 Cor. 13:1-13) should leave no-one in doubt about the great importance the apostle attached to loving neighbours.

In addition Paul was convinced that good behaviour depended on sound beliefs. The fact that men had exchanged the truth of God for wrong belief or, as he put it, a lie, had produced all kinds

135

of error and evil (Rom. 1:24-32). Similarly he argued that abandonment of belief in resurrection produces moral licence – those with no thought of being raised to face judgment say, 'eat and drink for tomorrow we die' (1 Cor. 15:32-34). The conviction that belief conditions behaviour is also shown by the way in which in many of his letters Paul followed doctrinal exposition with ethical exhortation (e.g., Rom. 12:1; Eph. 4:1; Col. 3:1). For him good behaviour is very much the product of belief in doctrines that are soundly biblical.

Sins to be avoided

The sins that worried the apostle are, in the main, listed with considerable repetition in four passages: Galatians 5:19-21; Romans 1:24-32; 1 Corinthians 6:9-10 and Ephesians 5:3-5. We can confine our study to these passages, in which Paul highlights both evil attitudes and evil actions and in which he picks up all his important emphases.

1. Sins of attitude
Like the Lord Jesus, Paul condemns attitudes which generate outward acts like murder, adultery, theft and slander. He sees men's hearts as filled with greed (covetousness), envy, deceit and malice (Rom. 1:29). He lists hatred (enmity), discord (a quarrelsome spirit), jealousy and fits of rage (uncontrolled anger) among the acts of the sinful nature (Gal. 5:20, AV, 'works of the flesh').

He regards those who have such attitudes as insolent, arrogant and boastful. He sees them as people who devise ways of doing evil, as inwardly heartless (devoid of natural affection) and ruthless (Rom. 1:29-31). In Romans 2:8 he calls all such persons 'self-seekers'.

2. Religious sins
For Paul the root of human sin lies in the erroneous beliefs and the consequent godlessness and idolatry of people, who at rock bottom are 'haters of God' (Rom. 1:18-23, 30). Listing what he calls 'the acts of the sinful nature' (Gal. 5:19-21) he includes:

(i) *Idolatry*. Idolatry is the worship of material objects, idols or images. Worshippers claim that they do not worship the idol itself but the spirit they regard as represented by it or as dwelling in it. A living human being, like the Roman emperor in the early Christian era, also became an idol when worship was directed to him or her rather than to the true God. The same can be true today in relation to popular heroes, whether politicians or pop stars. In addition any activity that, to the exclusion of other affections, becomes the dominating passion of a person's life can be that person's focus of worship, his or her idol. Anything or anyone that takes the place of the Lord or comes between a person and him is an idol and makes the person concerned an idolater.

ii) Witchcraft. The apostle rejects as wicked the whole gamut of occult activity, including resort to sorcery, spells, divination and magic whether the intention is to help or harm others (Gal. 5:20). He had encountered witchcraft on his missionary journeys (Acts 13:4-12; 19:17-20) and saw it as a serious offence against God, whose honour and sole sovereignty it challenged (thus breaking the first commandment) and whose name it sometimes even dared to invoke in contravention of the third commandment.

3. Sexual sins

In the Roman world in which Paul ministered adultery, prostitution, divorce and homosexual practices were common. The emperor, Julius Caesar is reputed to have been what is now called 'bi-sexual' – 'every woman's man and every man's woman!' The fact that folk with a background of these sins had been converted and brought into the churches (1 Cor. 6:11) made it imperative that he speak firmly about such sins. He had to warn the converts against continuing with, or falling into, practices which could mar their lives and damage the witness of the churches.

Writing to Corinth he dealt with a disturbing case of incest such as did not, he said, even occur among pagan people (1 Cor. 5:1). This was so serious that the offender was to be denied the benefits of Christian fellowship. He also warned against prostitution and all forms of sexual immorality (1 Cor. 6:12-20). Since immorality was very common he even added a plea in favour of marriage and against the single state he himself preferred (1 Cor. 7:2, cf. vv. 26, 32-35).

Each of Paul's four lists of sins begins with sexual immorality, which must have been the major danger to the early believers. Every form of sexual immorality – harlotry, fornication, impurity or sexual vice and debauchery (unrestrained sexual activity or licentiousness) – was rejected as activity of the sinful nature (Gal. 5:19).

Unconventional use of the human body, including male and female homosexual acts, is specified as unacceptable and evil behaviour (Rom. 1:24-27; 1 Cor. 6:9b). However, while Paul was strongly opposed to homosexual acts, he did not regard them or any other sexual sin as beyond God's forgiveness. He could genuinely say to the Corinthians, 'that is what some of you were. But you were washed, you were sanctified, you were justified...' (1 Cor. 6:11). In his mind the Lord had delivered the homosexuals to whom he was referring from their homosexual practices.

4. Socially disruptive sins

Paul's lists of sins include dissension – a standing apart and isolating of oneself for selfish reasons – and factions – a choosing of one's own line of belief or action so as to separate oneself from others in a sectarian fashion. Again Corinth provided a glaring example as the believers had become divided through loyalty to different leaders – 'I follow Paul, I follow Apollos' (1 Cor. 1:10).

To these we can add from Galatians 5:21 and 1 Corinthians 6:10, *disobedience to parents*, *drunkenness*, and *orgies* (wild unrestrained feasting often involving sex as well as food and drink), *thieving*, *slandering* (defaming others) and *swindling* (i.e., obtaining money by cheating). All of these sins had, and continue to have, a disruptive effect on the social order.

Motives to be adopted

Against the background of such sinfulness Paul makes several strong appeals to his readers. He asks them to realise that the Christian ethic is the only appropriate way of life for those who profess to follow Christ. This means that the individual's motives must be in line with that ethic. It means that each Christian must always:

1. Endeavour to heed divine revelation

Paul used those laws of the Old Testament that were endorsed and re-affirmed by Christ. His insistence on abstinence from murder, adultery, theft and coveting arise both from the ten commandments and from Jesus. The ideal of lifelong commitment in marriage is based both on Genesis 2:24 and on our Lord's opposition to wrongful divorce. The requirement to obey parents (Eph. 5:31; 6:1-3) arises from the fifth commandment and from our Lord's own example. The apostle's strong insistence on giving care to enemies reflects what our Lord taught in Matthew 5:46 and Luke 6:27. At Miletus (Acts 20:35) he quoted an otherwise unknown saying of the Lord – 'It is more blessed to give than to receive.'

In addition Paul often urged his readers to imitate the ways of God and of the Lord Jesus – 'be imitators of God ... live a life of love as Christ loved us and gave himself up for us' (Eph. 5:1, cf. Phil. 2:5: 'Your attitude should be the same as that of Christ Jesus'). Their behaviour was to be patterned on that of the Saviour while he was on earth and on that of the Father, the Sovereign Lord, in heaven. Similarly the apostle was concerned that his friends in Colossae would allow 'the word of Christ' to dwell in them richly, and that, whatever they did, they would do in the name of and, therefore, in harmony with the teaching of the Lord Jesus (Col. 3:16-17).

2. Fear damaging consequences

Many people today dislike the idea of fear as a motive for good behaviour. They point out that it can lead to hypocrisy and to a 'goodness' that only lasts as long as the emotion of fear persists. While there is indeed such a risk, fear is not necessarily an unworthy motive. It can and often does contribute to repentance before God and thereafter to consistent Christian living.

Preaching at Mars Hill in Athens Paul warned that God would

judge the world (Acts 17:30-31). Writing to the Galatians he warned that men reap what they sow and should, therefore, fear the consequences of the way they live (Gal. 6:7-8). Later, writing to the Christians in Rome, he affirmed that ultimately – 'on the day when God will judge men's secrets through Jesus Christ' – each person will be rewarded 'according to what he has done' (Rom. 2:16, 6). In a similar vein he told the Corinthians that, even as Christians, they would face judgment and evaluation of their works. In that day, he said, some would suffer loss and would only be saved as escapees from fire or as we might say today, 'by the skin of their teeth'.

Divine judgment is indeed to be feared and dare not be ignored. Fear of it is surely a proper motive for turning from sin and evil to righteousness and good behaviour.

3. Seek good consequences

For Paul, disciplined living under the law of Christ will produce good consequences. While one's main motivation must be to do what is right, one must also seek good consequences. For example:

• *The satisfaction and honour of God.*
The Christian's supreme aim must be to ensure, as far as in him lies, that God is glorified (Rom. 15:6,7, 1 Cor. 10:31).

• *The good of neighbours.*
Fellow Christians are to be benefited by acts of care and kindness (Rom. 13:8-10; 15:2-3; 1 Cor. 10:23; 14:26; Eph. 4:25, 29) and so are unbelievers (Gal. 6:9; 1 Tim. 2:1). Put negatively this means doing no harm to neighbours (Rom. 13:10) and making sure that no example is set that would lead a neighbour astray (1 Cor. 8:9ff.).

• *The upbuilding of the Church.*
The gifts a Christian receives from God are given in order to strengthen both individuals and local churches in the faith (Rom. 12:3-8; 1 Cor. 12:12-31; 14:26; Eph. 4:7-13).

• *The well-being of oneself.*

While self is not to be the primary motivation of the Christian life, one's own well-being is not to be neglected. Neither is it excluded by the command, which requires us to love our neighbours *as we love ourselves.* We have, in fact, a duty to look to ourselves (Gal. 6:1) and to build our lives on values that will survive the test of judgment. Because the believer is the dwelling place, the temple, of the Holy Spirit he is responsible to care for that temple and to avoid anything that physically, emotionally, morally or spiritually would damage or destroy it (1 Cor. 3:12-17).

Virtues to be pursued

1. Good inner attitudes

Paul expects the attitudes of those who follow Christ to be transformed from those that arise through the selfishness that is natural to us to those that express holiness and please God (Rom. 12:1-2). He follows this with an important priority – that believers should not think of themselves more highly than they ought or, in other words, that they should not value themselves and their abilities above their real worth (Rom. 12:3, 4). In parallel with this he exposed and condemned the arrogant pride of Christians at Corinth and told them that, while knowledge (the thing they claimed to have) 'puffs up,' love (the quality they lacked) 'builds up' (1 Cor. 8:1, cf. 1 Cor. 4:6-21; 1 Tim. 3:6).

The ninefold 'fruit of the Spirit' (Gal. 5:22-23) provides a good basic picture of the kind of person Paul wanted his readers to be. The nine words represent not nine different and separable fruits but one fruit which expresses itself in nine different ways, each of which ought to characterise the life of every Christian.

The fruit of the Spirit entails:

• *love*. The focus is on an unconquerable benevolence to others. It is wonderfully described in 1 Corinthians 13:4-7: 'Love is patient, love is kind ...'

• *joy*. This is inward delight based on one's blessings in Christ.

• *peace*. In the New Testament, peace embraces the significance of the Hebrew *shalom* and points to a calm serenity and a sense of well-being through knowing God's love and care and through expressing that care to others.

• *patience*. This is forbearance and fortitude in the face of opposition and suffering.

• *kindness*. This is a goodness of heart that will not offend but rather seek to benefit others.

• *goodness*. This word points to a way of life that goes beyond mere conformity to a standard of right. A good life is marked by integrity and the avoidance of anything that would cause hurt to others.

• *faithfulness*. This simply means trustworthiness and complete reliability.

• *gentleness*. The reference is to a meekness of spirit that makes a person teachable and acceptive of correction and discipline.

• *self-control*. The Greek word means having mastery over one's desires and one's indulgence in pleasure, possessions, position or power.

In Philippians 4:8 Paul calls for his readers' thoughts to be concentrated on what is morally excellent and truly worthy of praise. As examples he mentions what is *true* (not devious or deceitful), *noble* (serious as opposed to frivolous or empty), *right* (i.e., by God's standards), *pure* (morally), *lovely* (loveable and love inspiring) and *admirable* (high-toned).

In addition the apostle was anxious that his readers should be *gentle* and *gracious* (Phil. 4:5; 1 Tim. 3:3; Tit. 3:2, cf. 2 Cor. 10:1). His concern seems to have been that they would express fairness, moderation and charity in their relationships with other people. In other passages he urged his readers to have a *forgiving spirit* toward one another – 'forgive as the Lord forgave you' (Col. 3:13, cf. 2 Cor. 2:7; Eph. 4:32).

2. Behaviour consistent with faith

The essential challenge of Paul's ethic is that Christians live in a manner worthy of or consistent with their calling and with the gospel. Their duty is to please the Lord by bringing to him a positive return as their lives bear fruit through good works (Eph. 4:1; Phil. 1:27; Col. 1:10; 1 Thes. 2:12). This entails 'putting off' or abandoning a former way of life and a 'putting on' of a new self patterned on the righteousness and holiness of God (Eph. 4:23-24).

In this new life truthfulness must replace falsehood, honest and useful work must replace stealing and helpful talk must replace unwholesome conversation (Eph. 4:25-29). Bitterness, rage, anger, brawling, slander and malice must be replaced by kindness and compassion (Eph. 4:31-32). There must be no sexual impurity, no obscene or coarse joking and no drunkenness but rather positive thanksgiving and worship of God. The follower of Christ is to 'live a life worthy of the Lord', pleasing 'him in every way, bearing fruit in every good work' and 'growing in the knowledge of God' (Col. 1:10).

3. Concern for social life and well-being

i) In relation to the state

The Roman world of the first century was marked by strong government, relative peace and a reasonable concern for justice. Paul had been able to avail himself of the protection offered by his Roman citizenship (Acts 22:25) and had no difficulty in urging his readers in Rome and elsewhere to submit to the authorities of the day and to pay taxes where taxes were due. He said, 'Everyone must submit himself to the governing authorities, for there is no authority except that which God has established' (Rom. 13:1-7; Tit. 3:1). He even urged Timothy to encourage the Christians at Ephesus to pray for rulers in the assurance that doing so is acceptable and pleasing to God (1 Tim. 2:1-2).

Clearly Paul knew that society needs the peace and stability which flows from strong governmental authority and, on the assumption that it acted 'as God's servant to do good' (Rom. 13:4), the Roman government had his support. Despite the fact that he had suffered greatly at the hands of civil authorities (2 Cor. 1:8-11; 11:23-33), the apostle was no social anarchist!

ii) In relation to marriage

Paul regarded marriage as a permanent relationship between one man and one woman as ordained by God at creation. He saw marriage as a protection against sexual immorality (1 Cor. 7:1-5). But because of pressures operating at the time he had a preference for the single life though on no account would he force celibacy on his readers. At the same time he insisted that, while desertion may sometimes have to be accepted, a Christian should not initiate the break-up of his or her marriage (1 Cor. 7:10ff). The bond was to be kept absolutely sacred.

The sacredness of marriage is further illustrated by the fact that Paul could use it as a picture of the relationship between Christ and his church (Eph. 5:21-32). In pursuing this he teaches that headship in marriage rests in the husband. However, in contrast to what went on in most societies, headship is presented as a benign arrangement that contributes to good social order and is to be governed by the husband's love for his wife and by her love and respect for him (Eph. 5:22-33; Col. 3:18-19).

iii) In relation to the family

The principles of headship and love are also to operate in family life. Children are to obey their parents 'in the Lord' – a qualification that could imply that respecting and obeying parents is a duty we owe to the Lord. It might also be understood as allowing older believing children to emerge from bondage to unbelieving or wicked parents who do not belong to the Lord and who do not live in a way that honours him.

At the same time fathers were told that they must not exercise their headship in a way that would exasperate or provoke their children or cause them to 'lose heart' (Eph. 6:1-4; Col. 3:20-21). In later life children have a duty to provide for their parents especially if they should happen to be widows (1 Tim. 5:3-8).

iv) In relation to servants

Associated with family relationships are those with servants, many of whom would have been slaves in Paul's day. Again the principle of authority benignly exercised and wholeheartedly obeyed is affirmed (Eph. 6:5-9; Col. 3:22-4:1).

At the same time Paul raises the master-slave relationship to a higher plane by asserting that in Christ there is 'neither slave nor free' (Gal. 3:28, cf. 1 Cor. 7:21-23). What this means is wonderfully illustrated in his advice to Philemon about how he should receive back Onesimus, his runaway servant, as a brother and no longer as a mere slave (Phm. 10-16). It is generally agreed that Paul's references to slaves not only call for good conditions of work but also undercut the whole institution of slavery. They led eventually to Christians taking action to end slavery.

v) In relation to the status of women

On the place of women in society Paul asserts that in Christ there is 'neither male nor female' (Gal. 3:28). He is saying that both sexes without distinction inherit the blessings of the gospel and that there is to be no discrimination against women any more than against Gentiles or slaves – 'all are one in Christ Jesus.' This was a dramatic change from the Jewish faith in which a man began each day by thanking God that he had not been born a Gentile, a slave or a woman!

vi) In relation to differences of race

Paul, like ourselves today, lived in a world seriously divided by racial and tribal differences. He says that in Christ there is neither Jew nor Greek (Gal. 3:28, cf. Eph. 2:14-16). He means that in the community of God's people differences of race have become irrelevant and all believers (i.e., Jews and the non-Jews who had become Christians) are one in Christ. This obligates Christians to accept believers of all races without discrimination and on equal terms with those of their own race.

Summing Up

As we read Paul's epistles we see that he calls for disciplined living. He repeatedly used three metaphors, each of which implies stringent training and total commitment by the believer himself.

• *the soldier*, who by virtue of his position must train and discipline himself for war and to obey orders (1 Cor. 9:7; 2 Cor. 10:2-6; Eph. 6:13-17; 1 Thess. 5:8).

• *the athlete,* who also must train and discipline himself and make sure that he knows and keeps the rules of any contest he might enter (1 Cor. 9:24-27; Phil. 3:14; 2 Tim. 4:7).

• *the steward*, who is trained to manage someone else's affairs and to keep the rules laid down by his master (1 Cor. 4:1-2; 2 Tim. 4:7).

As the end of his life drew near, Paul could tell Timothy that he himself had been a good soldier, a persevering athlete and a faithful steward.

I have fought the good fight (the soldier), I have finished the race (the athlete), I have kept the faith (the steward) (2 Tim. 4:7).

For Paul, supreme human discipline is not enough. True godliness needs the presence and power of the Holy Spirit, who is the vital power for the Christian life (Rom. 8:1-27). Each Christian must seek to live constantly under his control. He says, 'Live by the Spirit, and you will not gratify the desires of the sinful nature' (Gal. 5:16, cf. Rom. 8:4; Gal. 5:16-26; Eph. 3:16).

It is the fruit of the Spirit – 'love, joy, peace, patience, kindness, goodness, faithfulness, gentleness and self-control' (Gal. 5:22f.) –and not mere human endeavour that marks a person who is living by the true biblical ethic.

13

The General Epistles

There are seven General Epistles, Hebrews, James, 1 and 2 Peter, 1, 2 and 3 John and Jude. They have considerable ethical content but much of it repeats features we have already encountered in the Gospels and in Paul's letters. It is only necessary, therefore, to focus briefly on the distinctive emphases of the main books.

The Epistle to the Hebrews

The writer of this letter is seeking to counteract a temptation facing Jewish believers of returning to Judaism. He does so by showing (1) the superiority of Christ over Moses and the priesthood of the Old Covenant and (2) the superiority of his work of atonement over the practices and institutions of Old Testament religion (chs. 1–10).

As is the case in many of Paul's letters doctrinal argument is followed by application of an ethical nature. Thus the worthies of Old Testament times, whose stories appear in chapter 11 are presented as men and women whose faith in God showed itself in their behaviour. Thus, for example, Noah built an ark and Abraham left Ur of the Chaldees to travel towards the land of promise even though he didn't know where it was (vv. 7,8). Later he acted out his faith when he obeyed God's command and went to Mount Moriah fully expecting that he would offer up his much loved son, Isaac, as a sacrifice (vv. 17-19). Similarly Moses made a choice to be identified with God's despised people and persevered in active service to God and to the people as he led them out of Egyptian bondage (vv. 24-29). The list goes on focusing on men and women who, in spite of hardship and persecution acted in accordance with what they believed. They showed their faith by their works.

On the basis of the example of these Old Testament heroes the writer appeals to his readers that they, surrounded in their Jewish traditions by so many faithful witnesses, abandon everything that could hinder their progress in the Christian life (12:1-17; 13:1-8). They must throw off every sin that marred their lives and every impediment that hindered their progress and must persevere in running the race that is the Christian life (12:1-2). He then asks them to think of the way in which Jesus had endured opposition and to see the example he had set as the basis for keeping themselves active in the Christian life and as a means of ensuring that they would not grow weary or lose heart (12:3).

Next he points out that hardship should be endured as a God-given discipline (12:7). It is meant for the good of the readers so that ultimately they might share in God's holiness and might produce a harvest of righteousness and peace – that they might live lives that accord with the Christian ethic (12:7-11). This means that they should live righteously and in peace with all men (12:14). It also means that they should allow no bitterness to develop among them to spoil their Christian fellowship (12:15).

In addition they must also ensure that no-one among them is sexually immoral or guilty of living in a godless way (12:16).

This is followed in chapter 13 with further ethically significant injunctions:

• *Love one another* (v.1). The tense of the verb is continuous – 'keep on loving ...' This applies our Lord's second greatest commandment, 'you shall love your neighbour as yourself,' to Christian fellowship.

• *Be hospitable to strangers* (v.2). Meeting the needs of and providing for 'strangers' was an obligation under the Old Covenant order (Exod. 22:21; Deut. 10:17-19). The Jewish recipients of this letter would be aware of their duty and should realise that the strangers might even be angels! The mention of angels is thought to be an allusion to the experience of Abraham and Sarah at Mamre (Gen. 18). However, the Greek word 'angel' (*angellos*) means messenger and could refer to human messengers, perhaps the representatives of other churches as is the case in Revelation 2 and 3 or even to itinerant preachers.

• *Be concerned for prisoners* (v.3). The writer is probably thinking of imprisoned believers who were being ill-treated. The readers were to think of such as if they themselves were in prison with them. Other prisoners may also be in view.

• *Be pure and faithful in marriage* (v.4). Marriage is an honourable estate and is not to be defiled by immorality.

• *Be financially content* (vv.5-6). Because God has promised to be present with and to help his people they can calmly rely on his provision. They (we) must therefore keep themselves (ourselves) 'free from the love of money'.

• *Be respectful of Christian leaders* (vv. 7,17). The faith of leaders, especially those through whom the readers had heard God's word, is to be imitated. Such leaders are also to be obeyed so that their work will be a joy to themselves and a benefit to all.

• *Be prayerful* (vv. 18,19). The readers are told that their prayers will contribute to the author's restoration to them. In effect such prayer is presented as a moral duty, as a matter of ethics.

The Epistle of James

James is primarily concerned with the Christian life. His letter reminds us that the Christian life becomes a sham if it is not marked by behaviour consistent with the profession of faith that has been made – 'faith without works' (i.e., consistent conduct) 'is dead' (2:14-26).

The letter has some sixty imperatives, many of which are followed by paragraphs expanding, illustrating and applying them. For example, the injunction, 'don't show favouritism' (2:1) is illustrated and developed in terms of the way the rich and the poor are often treated when they appear at meetings. The rich man gets a great amount of attention while the poor man is discriminated against by being shunted into a less conspicuous place (2:2-13).

1. James' view of goodness

James' great concern is that Christians should keep 'the royal law', i.e., that they love their neighbours as they love themselves (2:8). The royal law (Greek, *nomon basilikon,* the law of the king/kingdom) is James' way of referring to what Paul calls 'Christ's law'. He expounds the implications of this in terms of listening before speaking or becoming angry (1:19-20), of being truly humble (4:6-10) and of replacing earthly wisdom (involving such harsh and unpleasant evils as jealousy and self-centred ambition) with qualities such as purity, sincerity, considerateness, submissiveness, impartiality and peace making (3:13-18).

Religion acceptable to God involves looking after orphans and widows (1:27). It also entails truthfulness, 'Yes' meaning 'Yes' and 'No' meaning 'No' (5:12). It requires an avoidance of the slander that results from judgmental attitudes (4:11-12) and demands a taming of the tongue (3:1-12). Patience in waiting for the Lord's return in face of suffering is encouraged – 'Be patient then, brothers, until the Lord's coming. See how the farmer waits for the land to yield its valuable crop …' (5:7-11).

2. James' catalogue of evils

In this epistle there are more imperatives aimed at stopping evil actions than there are in favour of good ones. The prohibitions are not, however, entirely negative – by saying what should not be done they reinforce the good James seeks to encourage.

Moral filth and prevalent evil (1:21) were general descriptions of the decadence of the time. Failure to do what the word (of God) says is a serious fault (1:22-27). Failure to control the tongue (1:26; 3:1-12) is an especially serious fault.

> If anyone considers himself to be religious and yet does not keep
> a tight rein on his tongue, he deceives himself and his religion is
> worthless (1:26).

Favouritism and boasting are also faults. Both provide James with further opportunity to display his superb powers of illustration, (2:1-13; 3:1-12). Boasting corrupts the boaster and words spoken by the tongue, like a spark, can start a fire of dislike and hatred that destroys good relationships.

James condemns an earthly wisdom that produces envy, selfish ambition, disorder and evil practices (3:13-17). He has no time for the covetous and pleasure-seeking motives that produce fights and quarrels (4:1-3). Uncaring attachment to material wealth (5:1-6) and unnecessary or light-hearted resort to oaths (5:12) are alike unacceptable.

The Epistles of Peter

Peter writes to encourage scattered believers (1Pet. 1:1) to live godly lives in a hostile society.

1. Their presentation of virtue

Peter urges obedience to the will of God and an eagerness to do what is right. He is concerned that his readers follow the example of Christ and pursue God's will – he left us 'an example, that you [we] should follow in his steps' (1 Pet. 2:21; cf. 1:1,14; 2:16; 3:13,17; 4:1,2).

Peter wants to see his readers loving each other deeply and providing hospitality and heartfelt care for each other (1 Pet. 1:22; 3:8; 4:8-9). He urges them, and his readers in subsequent generations, to serve each other in the strength God provides (1 Pet. 4:10,11).

The apostle is acutely aware of the fact that his readers had already faced and would continue to face opposition because of their faith. He therefore wants them to live such good lives before non-Christians that their accusers will notice and be led to give praise to God (1 Pet. 2:12). But, since there is no guarantee that their oppressive situation will change, he urges them to rejoice in the fact that they are sharing in the sufferings of Christ. They should regard insult for the sake of Christ as a great blessing and as evidence that the Spirit of God and of glory was resting on them (1 Pet. 4:12-14).

Peter, like James, is not happy with a faith that fails to produce virtue. So he asks his readers to make every effort to add to their faith a whole series of virtues – 'goodness, knowledge, self-control, perseverance, godliness, brotherly kindness and love' (2 Pet. 1:5-7). These qualities overlap to a considerable degree Paul's description of the fruit of the Spirit – 'love, joy, peace, patience, kindness, goodness, faithfulness, gentleness and self-control' (Gal. 5:22f). For Peter such virtues are the key to effective and productive growth in the knowledge of Christ. At the same time their absence is evidence of spiritual blindness and of a person having forgotten that he had been cleansed from his past sins, that is to say, it is evidence of backsliding (2 Pet. 1:8,9).

2. Their inventory of vices

Peter mentions a great variety of evils, most of which we have encountered already. At one point he focuses on pagan debaucheries in which his readers had indulged in the past and from which they may not yet, perhaps, have been fully delivered (1 Pet. 4:3). He mentions 'lust' (longings for forbidden things), 'drunkenness' (wine bubbling up and overflowing), 'orgies' (wild indulgences of the appetites, whether of food, drink or sex), 'carousings' (drinking bouts) and 'idolatry'. He notes that other people ('they', meaning, we can assume, non-Christians with whom his readers had previously cavorted) couldn't understand why his readers were now avoiding the dissipation in which they participated. Because of this they, their former companions, were heaping abuse on the Christians (v. 4).

Peter's concern is that his readers should abandon such misdemeanours and adopt the attitudes of Christ – 'since Christ suffered in his body, arm yourselves with the same attitude.' His vision is that they would live the rest of their lives in accordance with the will of God rather than according to their own evil human desires (v. 2).

3. Their directions about social life

i) in relation to the state

Christians are urged to submit to and honour all those in authority over them, whether the king himself (the Roman emperor, Caesar) or those appointed to act as governors under him. They are reminded that God's will is that they do good in the context of civil life so that the criticisms of those who persecuted them might be silenced. Their freedom in Christ must not be a cover-up for evil. They must live as 'servants of God' (1 Pet. 2:13ff.).

ii) in relation to servants and masters
Again submission is required even when a master is harsh and the servant has to suffer because of good he has done. God, says the apostle, 'is pleased with you when, for the sake of your conscience, you patiently endure unfair treatment' (1Pet. 2:19, NLT).

iii) in relation to marriage
A wife should submit to her husband and should have an inward rather than a mere external beauty – 'a gentle and quiet spirit'. His hope is that if any wife has a husband who as yet is not a believer he might be won over not by the words but by the behaviour of the wife. Their actions would speak louder than their words! For their part husbands are instructed to be thoroughly considerate of, and respectful to, their wives (1 Pet. 3:1-7).

iv) in relation to fellow believers
In this relationship harmony, sympathy, love, compassion and humility are needed (1 Pet. 3:8-12). Those in leadership as elders must live exemplary lives and display a spirit of enthusiastic and self-effacing service. They must not allow themselves to be dominated by a greedy pursuit of money but should rather give themselves in willing service looking to receive their reward when the Chief Shepherd appears (1 Pet. 5:1-6).

Young men are instructed to be submissive to those who are older. This may mean submission to older and more experienced men in general or submission to those holding office as elders (1 Pet. 5:5a).

In more general terms the apostle tells all his readers that they are to clothe themselves with humility towards one another because God resists the proud and gives grace to the humble (v. 5b,c). The implication is that young and old, rich and poor, established believers and new converts were to respect each other and rather than lording it over others be humbly submissive in relation to each other.

4. Their emphasis on motivation
Peter pleads for full commitment and eager zeal in the pursuit of what is good (1 Pet. 2:11-12; 3:13; 2 Pet. 3:14) and in the rejection of evil (1 Pet. 2:11; 5:9). He sets out three factors, which he believes should act as incentives to good behaviour:

i) seeking to conform to God's character.
'Be holy, because I am holy' (1 Pet. 1:16) is the key injunction. Christians are to arm themselves with Christ's attitudes, follow in his steps and behave properly for his sake (1 Pet. 2:13-17, 21; 2:13, 4:1).

ii) expecting personal blessing.
The Christian is not to repay evil with evil but with 'blessing'. It is to such a response that the believer has been called. Obedience to this command carries the promise of blessing for the one who does good (1 Pet. 3:9-14, citing Ps. 34:12-16).

iii) preparing for the Lord's return.
The coming day of the Lord demands self-discipline, mutual love and sincere Christian service (1 Pet. 4:7-11). The prospect of the material universe dissolving raises a question about behaviour – 'what kind of people ought you to be?' The answer is that Christians should be living holy and godly lives and seeking to be spotless, blameless and at peace with him (2 Pet. 3:11-14).

5. Their insistence on the work of God's Spirit
Human effort, however zealous, is not enough. Peter links our obedience to Christ with the sanctifying work of the Holy Spirit (1 Pet. 1:2). The word of God by which the Christian has been born anew and by which he purifies himself must also be involved (1 Pet. 1:22, cf. Ps. 119:9).

Human effort and divine power come together when Peter mentions the devil's onslaught on his readers. 'Be self-controlled and alert ... and the God of all grace will make you strong, firm and steadfast' (1 Pet. 5:8-10). 'To him', he adds, 'belongs the power for ever and ever' (v.11). As has been said, 'the Christian life and its progressive sanctification demands not fifty but one hundred percent of God and not fifty but one hundred percent of me!'

In 2 Peter that power becomes the basis of an appeal for a diligent effort to develop effective and productive lives (2 Pet. 1:3,4). It gives us everything we need for godly living but, nonetheless, the Christian must zealously add to his faith goodness and knowledge. He must develop self-control and perseverance and express his faith in acts of kindness and love.

The Epistles of John

In the Epistles of John the writer's prescriptions for Christian living have a double thrust. They ask believers to:

1. Live under the control of God's word

John says that, if we walk in the light, as he (God) is in the light, 'we have fellowship with one another and the blood of Jesus, his Son, purifies us from all sin' (1 John 1:7). The blessings of fellowship with the Father and the Son (v. 3) and of purification from all our sins are promised to those who let the light of God's revealed truth, that is, his spoken and written word, rule their lives. The reverse side of this is that those who claim to have fellowship with God but are not controlled by the light of his word and who do not do what he commands, are living a lie rather than living in and by the truth. Their profession of faith is a lie! (1 John 1:6; 2:4).

John goes on to say that those who obey God's commands experience his love to the full and find in that experience convincing evidence that their lives are truly rooted in God (2:5). As such they have an example to follow – 'Whoever claims to live in him must walk as Jesus did' (2:6). At this point John must have remembered our Lord's own words, 'I have set you an example that you should do as I have done for you' (John 13:15).

2. Love one another.

John is known as the apostle of love. He uses the unique New Testament Greek word for love, *agapë*, 21 times in these epistles. Repeatedly he presents 'love for one's brother' not just as a command but as evidence of the reality of one's Christian experience. He says that anyone who lives in the light, that is, under the control of God's word, does in fact love his brother (1 John 2:9,10, cf. 3:11; 4:7,21; 5:1-2; 3 John 4-6).

Absence of such love for one's fellows is evidence of a lack of love for God and of serving the devil (1 John 3:10; 15-16; 4:20-21). John goes as far as to say that anyone who does not love is still in a state of spiritual death and that anyone who does not love a brother is a murderer! (3:15). This is strong language and obviously reflects our Lord's words in the Sermon on the Mount – 'anyone who murders will be subject to judgment. But I tell you that anyone who is angry with his brother will be subject to judgment' (Matt. 5:21,22). Anger and hatred amount to virtual murder and in God's eyes call for judgment. This must ever stand as a stark warning to Christians.

For this apostle love for fellow-believers is evidence of a real relationship with God; while hatred of a brother is evidence of walking in darkness and of being a servant of Satan (2:11, cf. 3:7-10). As he says:

> Whoever loves his brother lives in the light ... Everyone who loves has been born of God and knows God (2:10; 4:7).

The Epistle of Jude

Jude scathingly condemns the evils of godless and immoral men (vv. 4, 8, 11), who had somehow managed to slip in among the believers. The chief sin of these men seems to have involved sexual immorality – they 'change the grace of our God into a licence for immorality and deny Jesus Christ our only Sovereign and Lord' (v.4). At the same time and, indeed, underlying their immorality, these were essentially self-centred individuals, who followed their own desires in order to gain advantages for themselves. Jude pronounces 'woe' on them because they have followed 'the way of Cain' (a path contrary to God's ways) and have *for the sake of profit* repeated the error of Balaam (v.11).

In response Jude urges his readers to build themselves up in their faith, to keep themselves in God's love, to be unselfishly merciful to others and to hate every taint of sinful corruption (vv. 2-23).

Conclusion
The general epistles endorse, then, the ethical emphases of the Gospels and the letters of Paul. They give expression to and re-iterate what Paul calls 'Christ's law' (1 Cor. 9:21) and what James terms 'the royal law' (Jas. 2:8). It is to observance of the ethical teachings of Christ that they call their readers.

14

Ethics in the Revelation

John, to whom the Revelation was given, was on the receiving end of Roman antagonism. He was a prisoner, a brother in suffering, on the island of Patmos (1:9). The visions he received were surely designed to assure him and other persecuted Christians that the Lord had not abandoned them. He was indeed on the throne and would ultimately judge those who opposed his work and persecuted his servants.

The Messages to the Seven Churches

1. Commendations

Six of the seven churches addressed by the Lord are commended for attitudes and actions of an ethical nature:

• *Ephesus* for hard work, for intolerance of wicked men and for endurance of hardships (2:2-3).

• *Smyrna* for bearing affliction and poverty (2:9).

• *Pergamum* for remaining faithful to the Lord in a Satan-dominated environment (2:13).

• *Thyatira* for love, faith, service and perseverance (2:19).

• *Sardis* for a few people who had remained pure (3:4).

• *Philadelphia* for keeping the Lord's word and commands despite lack of strength (3:8,10).

  • [*Laodicea* alone received no commendation.]

2. Rebukes
Five churches are rebuked for weaknesses or outright sin.

• *Ephesus* for a loss of devotion to the Lord. Their disobedience was ethical failure (2:4-6).

• *Pergamum* for tolerating idolaters and sexually immoral people. There were those who were subtly misleading Christians in the way similar to that by which Balaam misled Israel centuries earlier (2:14, cf. Num. 22-24). There were also Nicolaitans, probably followers of someone called Nicolas, who might even be the person of that name mentioned in Acts 6:5. Many scholars link them closely with those who followed Balaam but they may have been a different group. Whoever they were, their teaching was out of harmony with biblical truth (2:15). It may have involved an emphasis on Christian liberty that excluded separation from evils, like idolatry and sexual immorality, evils that were part and parcel of life and of pagan religion in Asia and the rest of the first century Graeco-Roman world.

• *Thyatira* for harbouring a woman claiming to be a prophetess but, in fact, practising harlotry (2:20-23).

• *Sardis* for being spiritually dead when they ought to have been alive (3:2-3).

• *Laodicea* for being lukewarm, relying on material wealth and not spiritual riches (3:15-18).

 • [*Smyrna* and *Philadelphia* are not rebuked]

The thrust of these messages is to urge faithfulness and perseverance in the Christian way no matter what the opposition of Satan or of secular authorities. Prominent in the Lord's appeals is the need for sexual purity, the lack of which was blighting at least three of the churches: Sardis, Pergamum, and Thyatira.

In the vision of the Lamb with the 144,000, John hears the glorified saints singing 'a new song' before God's throne in heaven.

The moral characteristics, by virtue of which they could be called 'blameless' in regard to their earthly lives, were that they had maintained sexual purity and had been truthful–no lies were found in their mouths (14:1-5).

The Conflict with Secular Power

The seven churches addressed in chapters 2 and 3 had begun to endure persecutions. In the visions that follow the persecution is pictured as becoming more intense.

1. Symbolic beasts from sea and earth

A 'beast' (almost certainly representing the Roman emperor) appears with authority bestowed by 'the dragon' (i.e., by Satan, 12:9). This beast has been wounded and as a result the 'whole world' follows him. His role is to make war on the saints by demanding that all the inhabitants of the earth worship him (13:7-8). Christians are told that they should willingly and, indeed, submissively accept their fate whether it was imprisonment or even death by execution – 'This calls for patient endurance and faithfulness on the part of the saints' (13:9-10).

A second beast then appears, looking like a lamb but essentially of the same type as the first, on whose behalf he operates (13:11-17). This beast seems to represent religious power and religious persecution. He orders the execution of all who refuse to worship the first beast. Harsh totalitarian rule is thus bolstered by state-affiliated religion. For John the focus was on the Roman Empire of his day and probably (or possibly) on its most famous persecuting emperor, Nero, whose name may be encoded in the number 666.

A subsequent vision focuses on the fall of 'Babylon the Great' (17:1-18:3). Most scholars believe that Babylon is also coded language for Rome and its empire. No doubt it also refers in more ultimate terms to the destruction of Satan and his kingdom.

2. A changed attitude to secular power

For our purpose the important ethical emphasis is the very obvious change in the attitude to the state which had developed in the short space of time that separated Romans 13 and Revelation 13-19. No doubt this change resulted from a change in the treatment of Christians by the state. They were now being persecuted rather than protected by the Roman Empire.

In consequence of this we have a triumphant taunt-song against Rome under the pseudonym, 'Babylon' (18:1-19:3). This displays considerable antagonism to the state and seems in opposition to the emphasis on submission to governing authorities taught by Paul (Rom. 13:1-7).

When the state behaves as God intended and works for the well-being of its citizens, the Christian can happily follow the instructions of Paul and Peter and can with integrity support it. But, when it acts as an agent of Satan and unjustly inflicts persecution on believers or on others, patient and passive endurance is called for. Instead of turning to violent resistance or revolution the Christian looks to the Lord for deliverance, possibly in this life but most certainly in the next.

In this book of the Revelation we do not have any reference to prayer for the emperor such as was requested by Paul (1 Tim. 2:1-4). Rather we have a hymn of praise to God because Babylon (i.e., the Roman Empire and/or a secular opposing government anywhere and in any age) is falling or has fallen. John actually portrays Rome as the mother of prostitutes being destroyed as God's salvation is made manifest (19:1-8).

This glorying over the fall of Babylon or Rome with its imprecatory language – 'give her back as she has given' (18:6-8) has sometimes been taken as encouraging revolutionary action against a bad government. But the reverse is the case, namely, that God's sovereign intervention alone is what brings down the oppressor and avenges the blood of his servants (19:1-3, cf. 7:14-17). The believer's proper response to persecution is one of patient submission and endurance.

The prospect of universal judgment

In what is usually known as the epilogue to the book (22:8-21) the fact of ultimate judgment is affirmed – 'Behold, I am coming soon! My reward is with me, and I will give to everyone according to what he has done' (v.12). Only those who wash their robes will have the right to enter the eternal city. Others, dogs (probably meaning wicked people), those who practise magic arts, the sexually immoral, the murderers, the idolaters and everyone who loves and practises falsehood, will be left outside (v.15).

That statement in itself thoroughly reflects and, indeed, gathers up much of the morality of the rest of the Bible. It shows that the Bible is a consistent whole. The evils condemned in Revelation are essentially the same as those condemned from the earliest times. And the same virtues of love for God and a hatred of wickedness are extolled.

Conclusion

The Book of Revelation effectively re-emphasises the overall biblical picture and calls for the same spirit of dedication to the moral standards, which God has been pleased to reveal to his people throughout the biblical period.

15

Living by the biblical ethic

Our Lord calls for wholehearted discipleship and challenges us to follow his own example and to be perfect as our Father in heaven is perfect (Matt. 5:48). The standard to which we are to conform is what Paul calls 'Christ's law'.

The law of Christ

1. Its basic commands

Our Lord's ethical teaching starts with his endorsement of the two basic absolute commands of the Old Testament. These require men to love the Lord, with their entire beings – 'with all your heart and all your soul and with all your strength' – and to love their neighbours as they love themselves.

As we saw earlier in these studies the two absolutes are expanded by the ten commandments, which emphatically also require love for God and love for other human beings.

• *Commands 1 to 4* demand respectively no other gods, no images representing God, no careless or false use of God's name and a proper reverence for his day. They tell us that God must have first place in our lives and that he will not share honour with any rival. Because Christ endorsed each of these commands we Christians, like the Israelites of old, are obliged to worship him and him alone.

• *The fourth* also calls for love towards neighbours by asking those in positions of authority to grant one day of rest each week to sons and daughters, to servants and even to working animals. It thus brings together and emphasises both love for God and love for one's fellows.

• *The fifth* commandment focuses on a human relationship, that of offspring to their parents. Parents are to be honoured and, in addition, loved and cared for as they become old or infirm. At the same time, since we all receive life from God through our parents, this commandment seems to recognise him as the source of life and to have something of a godward as well as a human dimension.

The remaining commands deal with specific relationships of human life and affirm what are called human rights.

• *The sixth* – 'You shall not murder' – forbids the individual from taking another person's life. It affirms that every human being has the most basic right of all, the right to life. In addition our Lord pointed out that the commandment also has an application to the inner life and puts antagonistic thoughts directed at another person virtually on a level with murder! (Matt. 5:21-26).

• *The seventh* – 'You shall not commit adultery' – forbids a sexual relationship with a person to whom one is not married. It protects marriage by giving every man and woman the right to a stable relationship without the fear of his or her spouse being illegitimately involved with someone else. It also safeguards family life and gives children the right to grow up in a wholesome environment without the tension and disruption caused by parental infidelity.

Jesus also brought inner thoughts into the picture. It is not just physical adultery that is wrong but inward lustful desires. He said that anyone who looks with lust in the heart has already become guilty of adultery, what we might call an inner or psychological adultery.

• *The eighth* – 'You shall not steal' – may have a primary application to kidnap and so confer on every individual person the right to freedom. But Scripture gives it a wider application that covers all stealing. It thus protects the right of each individual to own property and not to be wrongfully deprived of what he or she owns.

• *The ninth* – 'You shall not bear false witness' – relates primarily to testimony given to a court in order to have an innocent person pronounced guilty or a guilty one pronounced innocent. But false witness also applies to ordinary day-to-day situations as people talk and pass on hints and rumours that damage other people's names and reputations. All such testimony deprives its victims of justice. By forbidding it, the ninth commandment gives each person a right to justice before the law and in the eyes of friends and neighbours.

• *The tenth* – 'You shall not covet' – gets at the heart of morality by putting the searchlight on selfish thoughts and motives. All too often we covet pleasure, possessions, position, power and a host of things we think will enrich us in some way. Covetousness is greed for gain and because it takes over and dominates our minds it becomes a supreme object in our affections. Paul was thus able to call it idolatry (Col. 3:5).

2. The virtues it enjoins
The law of Christ includes the eight qualities of life set forth in the Beatitudes (Matt. 5:3-10). It also includes the great virtues he extolled – humility, integrity, readiness to forgive, stability in marriage and family life and care of the underprivileged. These qualities and virtues were repeated by Paul and the other apostolic writers and provide a pattern for Christian living in every age and in every cultural environment. Paul's presentation of the 'fruit of the Spirit' summarises: 'love, joy, peace, patience, kindness, goodness, faithfulness, gentleness and self-control.'

Like Paul and his colleagues, we are *under Christ's law*.

3. The principles it provides
Alongside these absolute commands the New Testament provides *principles* to guide Christians when they have to make decisions about matters not precisely covered by absolute commands. These

principles are, in fact, part of the law of Christ. They require us to use our minds to ensure that we do to others what we would like them to do to us (the Golden Rule, Matt. 7:12). They require us to do everything in ways, and with such motives, as will glorify God (1 Cor. 10: 31). They also demand that we consider the effect of what we do on our neighbours and especially the effect on a brother or sister whose faith is weak – we are not to be the cause of anyone stumbling (1 Cor. 10:32). We are to work for the well-being and upbuilding of others.

The biblical ethic also censures our careless failure to produce good actions. Paul, for example, speaks of the fact that we all *come short* of the glory of God (Rom. 3:23). He is using the Old Testament concept of sin as a matter of missing a target or failing to attain to a standard of behaviour. Like an arrow that falls short, our behaviour offends God by failing to attain the standards he has set for us. As James puts it, 'knowing the good and not doing it is sin' (James 4:17). When we are aware of a need in someone else's life and are able to do something to help, we are duty-bound to act in a way which will meet that need. Failure to do so is sin.

Power for Christian living

How, we ask, can Christians maintain a lifestyle consistent with this demanding ethic? The question is important because Christians often fail to appropriate the resources God has provided for them and as a result dishonour his name. What then are the priorities?

1. An enlightened conscience

The priority, surely, must be to educate our minds and consciences in *the law of Christ*. If we are to know and do what God requires, we must first know what the Scriptures teach. Our studies should at least have started us on the road to acquiring that knowledge. But let none of us ever think that we have learned it all and don't need to study the Scriptures any more! Till the day we die and pass into eternal glory we need to keep filling our minds with divine instruction and to be ever willing to be rebuked and corrected by that teaching. We must be diligent in studying *the word* and so equip our consciences to guide us ethically.

2. A strengthened will

It is not enough just to know the facts of what the Bible teaches about right and wrong. It is not enough to have an enlightened conscience and to try to do what it demands. We are inherently weak-willed and so fail to do what we know to be right. It is even possible that because of our sinful and selfish natures we may not even want to do what we know to be right! With Paul, we even do things which inwardly we hate – we can't carry out the good we want to do but instead do the evil we don't want to do! The sin in us weakens our wills and makes us do evil (Rom. 7:14-20).

We need help to strengthen our wills and drive us to right thinking and right action. While we need to put all our own energies into the task of living godly lives, we need God's strength alongside and controlling our efforts. We need a power that adds to our own strength and inclines our wills to do what is right and then enables us to do it.

Paul could encourage the Philippians to work out their own salvation with fear and trembling (i.e., make their own efforts but without pride or self-confidence). In doing so he could assure them that God was at work within them to enable them to will (i.e., to have desires etc.) and to act in ways that would please him. (Phil. 2:12,13). Knowing these things in his own experience Paul could even say, 'I can do all things through Christ who strengthens me' (Phil. 4:13).

And those words come to us today. If we put one hundred per cent of our energies into the task of living in God's way, we can trust him to work within us to strengthen our wills, to keep us from falling (Jude 24). And we can trust him to bring us in his good time safely to his eternal kingdom (2 Tim. 4:18).

3. Control by the Holy Spirit

In the teachings of Jesus and his apostles the source of such strengthening is a person, the person of the Holy Spirit. And God has sent that person – the Spirit of his Son – into the hearts of all true believers (Gal. 4:6).

Jesus promised that the Holy Spirit would teach his disciples and remind them of all that he had taught them (John 14:26). In saying this our Lord surely acknowledged that in our weaknesses and in the complexities of life we would easily forget his teachings on ethical matters and would need to be reminded of them. The Spirit, given as an abiding comforter or strengthener, must then be God's agent to prick our consciences and to help us behave in accordance with the biblical ethic. He even prevents those who yield control of their lives to him, who live in or by the Spirit, from fulfilling the desires, the lusts of the flesh, i.e., of the sinful nature (Gal. 5:16).

Our Christian duty is to live 'by the Spirit' and to walk with or be guided by him (Gal. 5:25). It is he who produces in our lives the great Christian virtues, the ninefold 'fruit of the Spirit' – love, joy, peace, patience, kindness, goodness, faithfulness, gentleness and self-control.

We must always be grateful for God's provision for us and especially for his presence with us through the Holy Spirit, who keeps us from following sinful lusts and enables us to grow into Christ's likeness. We can't emphasise the truth of God's keeping power or conclude these studies in biblical ethics with better words than those of the great doxology at the end of the Epistle of Jude:

To him who is able to keep you from falling and to present you before his glorious presence without fault and with great joy – to the only God our Saviour be glory, majesty, power and authority, through Jesus Christ our Lord, before all ages, now and for evermore! Amen.

Study Questions

Chapter 1 Ethics Today

(a) What are the essential differences between fittingness and consequentialist theories of ethics?

(b) What are the benefits and dangers of allowing the consideration of consequences to determine our actions?

Chapter 2 The Backdrop of Biblical Ethics

(a) How does an appreciation of the multifaceted nature of sin affect one's understanding of Christian ethics?

(b) What is the connection between salvation and ethics?

Chapter 3 Approaching Biblical Ethics

(a) Is there such a thing as a universal moral order? If so, how may we discover it?

(b) How may Christian ethics be classified and why?

(c) How are biblical ethical principles to be applied today?

Chapter 4 The Early Old Testament Period

(a) What are the creation ordinances and what guidance do they provide for us today?

(b) What can be learned from the Old Testament about the morality of the patriarchal period?

(c) What are the main categories of the Mosaic Law?

Chapter 5 The First Five Commandments

(a) What do the first five commandments teach us about worship and work?

(b) How may the Sabbath principle be applied today?

(c) In the light of the fifth commandment how should children treat their parents?

Chapter 6 The Second Five Commandments

(a) Is all killing prohibited by the sixth commandment?

(b) What bearing do the second five commandments have upon the well being of society?

(c) How does the ninth commandment enshrine the right to justice?

Chapter 7 The Prophets as ethical teachers

(a) What are the main emphases of the prophets?

(b) Did the message of the prophets apply only to Israel or is there evidence that it had a wider application?

(c) How relevant is the message of the prophets in today's world?

Chapter 8 The ethics of the Hebrew Sages

(a) How does the moral teaching of the Wisdom literature relate to the Ten Commandments?

(b) How does the Book of Proverbs teach about discipline?

(c) How does the Book of Job challenge the 'health and wealth' teaching of today?

Chapter 9 The First Century Scene

(a) In what ways do New Testament ethics build on the ethical teaching of the Old Testament?

(b) What are the main characteristics of New Testament ethics?

Chapter 10 Jesus as an ethical teacher (1)

(a) In what ways did Jesus see himself as fulfilling the Law?

(b) 'Jesus turned the law inwards'. Discuss.

Chapter 11 Jesus as an ethical teacher (2)

(a) What according to Jesus is virtue?

(b) What vices did Jesus condemn?

Chapter 12 Paul's Pattern for Christian Living

(a) 'Good behaviour depends on sound beliefs.' What evidence for this statement is there in the teaching of Paul?

(b) What motives should govern Christian behaviour?

(c) In what ways does Paul's teaching relate to the Christian as citizen?

Chapter 13 The General Epistles

(a) What are the main ethical emphases in the Epistle of James?

(b) 'Peter is not happy with a faith that fails to produce virtue.' Discuss.

Chapter 14 The Revelation

(a) In what ways is the state seen in a different light by John than it is by Paul? Why the difference?

(b) How should Christian believers react to persecution?

SUBJECT INDEX

SCRIPTURE INDEX

185